Painting Sign:

Collyer

ETTORE MAIOTTI

The Watercolor Handbook

Learning from the Masters

Clarkson N. Potter, Inc./Publishers
DISTRIBUTED BY CROWN PUBLISHERS, INC.
NEW YORK

ACKNOWLEDGMENTS

I wish to thank the artist Anna Pavesi for her help and for allowing me to reproduce in this book the various stages of one of her watercolors.
I am also grateful to Aldo Raimondi for permission to publish some of his works, which are masterpieces of the watercolor technique.
Finally, I should like to thank the firms Maimeri and Winsor & Newton for providing materials, and Marina Brizi and Luisa Violi for their valuable cooperation in the book's editing.

Those watercolors not otherwise cited are those of Ettore Maiotti

English translation copyright © 1986 by Gruppo Editoriale Fabbri, S.p.A.

Copyright © 1985 by Gruppo Editoriale Fabbri, S.p.A.

Copyright © 1985 by A.D.A.G.P., Paris, for the work of André Planson

Copyright © 1985 by Cosmopress, Geneva, for the work of Paul Klee

Translated by Michael Summers

Published in 1986 by Clarkson N. Potter, Inc., 225 Park Avenue South, New York, New York 10003.

Originally published in Italy as *Manuale pratico di acquerello* by Gruppo Editoriale Fabbri, S.p.A.

CLARKSON N. POTTER, POTTER, and colophon are trademarks of Clarkson N. Potter, Inc.

Manufactured in Italy

Library of Congress Cataloging-in-Publication Data

Maiotti, Ettore
The watercolor handbook

Translation of: Manuale pratico di acquerello.
1. Watercolor painting - Technique. I. Title.
ND2420.M3513 1986 751.42 2 86-633
ISBN 0-517-56306-1
10 9 8 7 6 5

First American Edition

CONTENTS

This beautifully produced and handy book is a boon to anyone wanting to learn more about painting in watercolor. Here you will discover what materials to choose, the basic techniques of color mixing and sketching, and tips on the sparing use of color. Useful exercises on particular subjects such as figures, landscapes, and animals are illustrated with the work of established watercolor painters, both old and contemporary.

Ettore Maiotti *first became interested in watercolors while he was studying frescoes; unable to find anyone to teach him to paint in watercolor, he taught himself. The personal style that he developed led to many commissions as an illustrator of books and magazines. There have been two one-man exhibitions of his work in Italy.*

INTRODUCTION

I first encountered watercolors many years ago when I was still a student of frescoes. At that time I was particularly drawn to the work of the Impressionists, and while I was studying these painters I came across some watercolors by Cézanne and one by Van Gogh (a small figure of a peasant woman) which I had not seen before. I was thunderstruck: I had fallen in love with watercolors.

I immediately set out to find a school where I could study this particular technique. To my dismay I found that, with the closing of the watercolor section of the Brera Academy in Milan (where Aldo Raimondi had taught) the teaching of this particular technique had apparently been abandoned. My friends know what I'm like when I get an idea into my head. I got hold of as many reproductions as possible of watercolors by the old masters to study them in depth. I bought a box of colors and began to work alone, trying to imitate the painting methods of the various artists and persevering until I had acquired a command of technique and formed a style of my own.

Meanwhile, artists and public alike were rediscovering watercolors. More recently, many young artists have turned to me for information and help; thus I decided to put together the results of my experiences in book form so they would be easily available to other would-be watercolorists.

I have described a number of different techniques allowing the student to select the one most suited to his or her style and purpose. In the initial exercises I have listed the colors required so as to establish the habit of working with the palette. In each of the exercises that follow I have shown the colors to be used and indicated whether they are to be used pure or mixed with others. There is no rule about using these particular colors, of course; suggestions are given to help the beginner faced with the problem of color-mixing. I have reproduced many watercolors of the old masters to show the wide range of techniques and help the student develop his or her own style.

Keep this book by you as you work. It has been specially designed to lie flat so that you can keep it open at the required page. Have it with you always, whether you are painting at home or outdoors.

Some of what you read in the following pages may not agree with the theories of other artists. Some watercolorists do not use a pencil but make their outlines with a brush charged with very diluted watercolor; others add color to finished pencil drawings. There is much debate among watercolorists about the merits of different approaches. My aim is not to champion a particular style but to show you several examples, analyze them and enrich them, with practical information.

Those who follow my suggestions and work hard, learning first the techniques of drawing and then of watercolor painting, persevering despite failures and consuming sheets of paper and quantities of paint, will eventually reach the stage when they have no further use for this book. They will have mastered the technique of painting in watercolor, and I will have achieved my aim.

Ettore Maiotti

MATERIALS NEEDED

Paper

Watercolor papers are made from shreds of cotton rag and are sold as rough, semi-rough, (known as "hot"), and "hot pressed" (with a very smooth surface and a slight sheen). Most watercolorists use the rough and semi-rough papers.

Preparing the paper

To prevent buckling when the wet paint is applied the paper must first be stretched.
Put the paper in a basin of water (fig. 1) or, if that is not possible, thoroughly wet it on both sides. Do not sponge the paper unless you have a very soft sponge. Then with a No. 8 sable-hair brush add a line of glue ½ in. (1 cm) wide along each edge of the underside (fig. 2). Now glue the paper to a frame or wooden board so that it adheres perfectly.

Glues

For thin paper: use a flour-based glue.
For thick paper: use an animal-based glue.
These are the best types of glue. However, if you do not have time to prepare them, you can use a vinyl-based glue instead.

Preparing a flour-based glue

Half-fill a tin, after washing it thoroughly, with plain white flour. Add water, pouring slowly and stirring continuously to prevent lumps from forming.
Bring a pan of water to the boil on a gas flame, put the tin in the pan and boil the mixture, stirring all the time until you smell the characteristic strong smell of flour. The glue is now ready.

Preparing an animal-based glue

This glue is generally obtained from minced rabbit skin which is soaked, boiled, filtered, and dried, and then sold in the form of transparent sheets or granules. Soak ¾ oz. (20 g) for 24 hours in ½ pt. (¼ liter) of cold water, then boil as above until completely dissolved. Use while still warm.

Gluing the paper to the board

Remember that the board must be a little bigger than the paper, which will be of the following standard measurements: A2, 16½ × 11¾ in. (420 × 297 mm); A3, 8¼ × 11¾ in. (210 × 297 mm); A4, 8¼ × 5⅞ in. (210 × 148 mm) and A5, 4 × 5⅞ in. (105 × 148 mm). First dampen the board. Then glue the paper to the board, pressing out the air bubbles with your hands. It will be ready to draw on when it has dried (fig. 3).

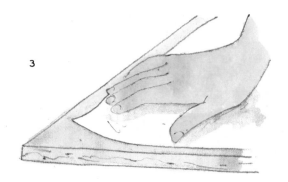

3

Drawing skill

The ability to draw, and thus to be able to sketch a design without hesitation, is very important in watercolor painting. A good watercolor is nothing more than a colored sketch: to paint a watercolor a minimum of color is necessary. The transparency and effects of great delicacy that can be obtained with tiny dabs of watercolor create an atmosphere often lacking in oil paintings.

Buying watercolors

Do not economize when buying watercolors: only with good quality paint can you be sure that the clarity of color will be maintained when the paints are diluted with water. Watercolors are sold in blocks, to be diluted with water (these are the most practical) (fig.

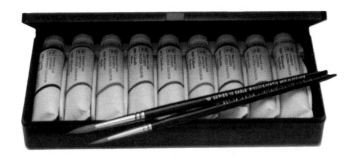

5

4

6

4) or, like tempera, in ready-to-use tubes (fig. 5). When you use the tubes arrange colors in

order on a ceramic or enamel tray (or even an ordinary white plate), starting with the warmest colors, and finishing with the coldest. Remember that the warm colors are yellow and red and the cold ones are green and blue.

I find that the boxes of watercolors in tablet form are the most practical (fig. 7). The

is sometimes a ring through which you can put your index finger so that the back of the hand can support the box while you paint (fig. 8). Before using this type of watercolor let a drop of water fall on each color.

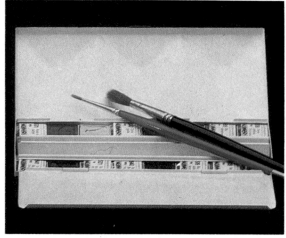

7

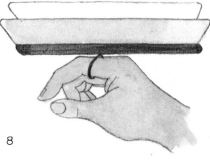

8

enamel lids can also serve as palettes. You can hold the box as in fig. 8 and paint quite comfortably, with enough water nearby to rinse the brushes. Underneath the box there

Useful hints
* Watercolor is a pigment to which a water dilutable gluing agent (such as honey or sugar) is added.
* The colors should be arranged on the palette starting with the warmest and finishing with the coldest in this order: yellow, orange, red, violet, blue, and green, and then the earth colors.
* Look at the colors as I have arranged them

Lemon Yellow	Chrome Deep	Rose Carthame	Carmine	Violet Carmine
Winsor Yellow	Cadmium Yellow	Cadmium Red	Rose Doré	Ultramarine Ash Blue
Cadmium Lemon	Indian Yellow	Cadmium Red Deep	Rose Madder Genuine	Manganese Blue
Chrome Lemon	Cadmium Yellow Deep	Vermilion	Cobalt Violet	Cobalt Blue
Aureolin	Cadmium Orange	Winsor Red	Permanent Mauve	Azure Cobalt
Chrome Yellow	Chrome Orange	Permanent Rose	Mauve	Cerulean Blue
Cadmium Yellow Pale	Bright Red	Rose Madder Alizarin	Winsor Violet	Permanent Blue
Gamboge	Cadmium Scarlet	Crimson Lake	Permanent Magenta	French Ultramarine
Aurora Yellow	Scarlet Vermilion	Alizarin Crimson	Purple Lake	Antwerp Blue
New Gamboge	Scarlet Lake	Alizarin Carmine	Purple Madder Alizarin	Winsor Blue

11

Prussian Blue · Viridian · Winsor Green · Burnt Sienna · Burnt Umber

Cyanine Blue · Olive Green · Cobalt Turquoise · Light Red · Warm Sepia

Indigo · Oxide of Chromium · Prussian Green · Venetian Red · Vandyke Brown

Winsor Emerald · Sap Green · Naples Yellow · Brown Madder Alizarin · Sepia

Terre Verte · Hooker's Green Light · Yellow Ochre · Indian Red · Davy's Gray

Cobalt Green · Hooker's Green Dark · Raw Sienna · Raw Umber · Charcoal Grey

in fig. 6. You will notice that black and white have not been included because they are very rarely used.

* Watercolor painting is a technique that requires the superimposing of transparent colors, starting with the lightest color and gradually adding the darker tones.

* If you need white, use the white of the paper.

* Never use black to darken the colors — it just makes them "dirty." Rather, add a touch of Vandyke Brown or Permanent Blue.

* Memorize the names of the colors. This will make it easier to arrange them on the palette and to buy new ones when necessary. On the following pages there are illustrations of the most commonly available watercolor boxes.

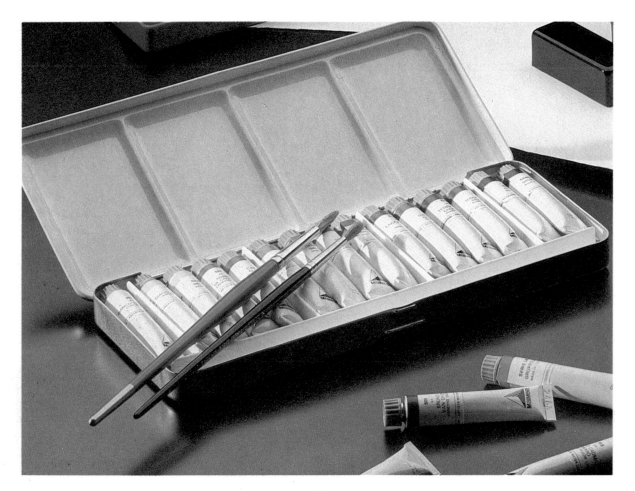

Sable-hair brushes

As with most high-quality products, it is the carefully controlled selection of its components that gives a brush its value. The most highly prized hair for painting in watercolors is sable hair.

This tradition of excellence in sable-hair brushes began in 1866 when Queen Victoria ordered Winsor and Newton to produce the best brush possible of her favorite size — No. 7. The brush was prepared by the most skilled craftsman with the best sable hair. The handle was made of ivory and the ferrule of pure silver. From then on brushes were made with handles of ivory and ferrules of metal (slightly less noble than silver) for other high-ranking customers.

Of course these brushes are very expensive, but if your work requires the best and you want a brush that will give you incomparable and long-lasting service, a sable-hair brush will be a worthwhile investment.

9 SERIES 7 FINEST SABLE WINSOR

8 SERIES 7 FINEST SABLE WINSOR & NEWTON

7 SERIES 7 FINEST SABLE WINSOR &

6 SERIES 7 FINEST SABLE WINSOR & NEWTON ENGLAND ■

5 SERIES 7 FINEST SABLE WINSOR & NEWTON ENGLAND ■

4 SERIES 7 FINEST SABLE WINSOR & NEWTON ENGLAND ▶

3 SERIES 7 FINEST SABLE WINSOR & NEWTON ENGLAND ■

2 SERIES 7 FINEST SABLE WINSOR & NEWTON ENGLAND ■

1 SERIES 7 FINEST SABLE WINSOR & NEWTON ENGLAND ■

0 SERIES 7 FINEST SABLE WINSOR & NEWTON ENGLAND ■

0.0 SERIES 7 FINEST SABLE WINSOR & NEWTON ENGLAND ■

000 SERIES 7 FINEST SABLE WINSOR & NEWTON ENGLAND ■

17

Synthetic or mixed-fiber brushes

Winsor and Newton have been producing a series of brushes which are nearer in quality to sable-hair brushes than any other synthetic brush.

The most important qualities of a watercolor brush are: a perfectly shaped tip; flexibility combined with a certain degree of rigidity; durability; and a capacity to hold the colors well.

To ensure a brush has these vital qualities a certain number of sable hairs must be used even in a synthetic brush.

The handle and the ferrule should be of good quality, with particular attention paid to the choke point of the ferrule. It is also important that the distance between the choke point of the ferrule and the handle is correct. If it is too short the ferrule may bend, letting water seep on to the handle; if it is too long the grasp may become uncomfortable. Either way the brush would soon be ruined.

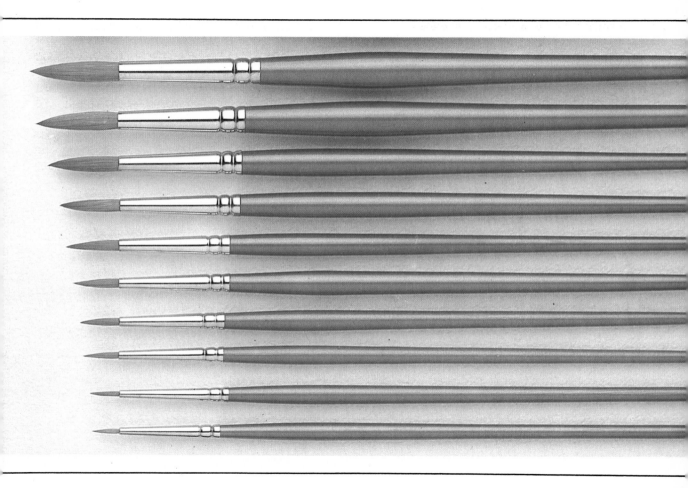

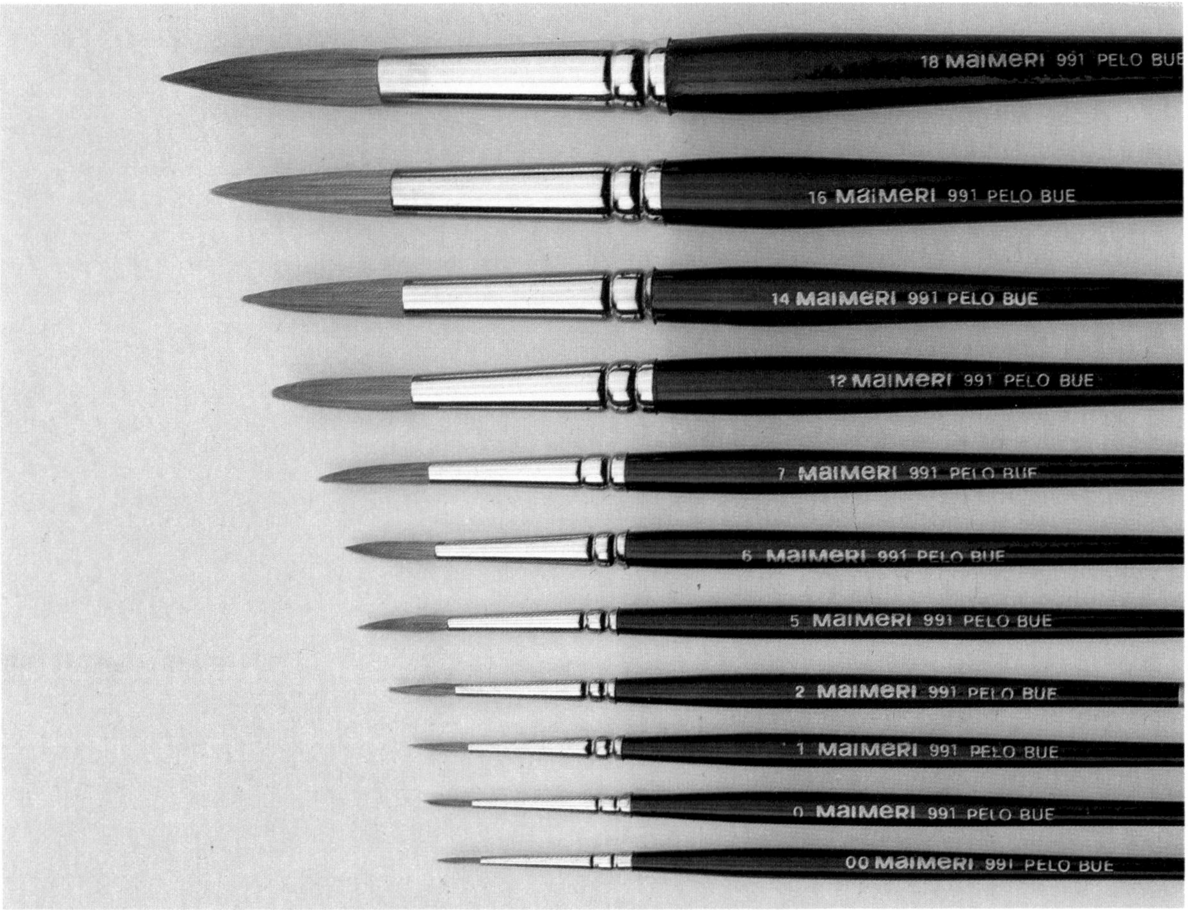

18 MaiMeRi 991 PELO BUE
16 MaiMeRi 991 PELO BUE
14 MaiMeRi 991 PELO BUE
12 MaiMeRi 991 PELO BUE
7 MaiMeRi 991 PELO BUE
6 MaiMeRi 991 PELO BUE
5 MaiMeRi 991 PELO BUE
2 MaiMeRi 991 PELO BUE
1 MaiMeRi 991 PELO BUE
0 MaiMeRi 991 PELO BUE
00 MaiMeRi 991 PELO BUE

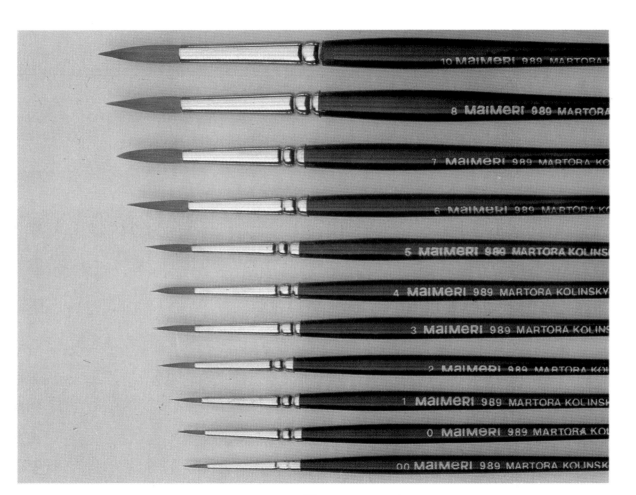

ANALYSIS OF A WATERCOLOR BY PAUL CEZANNE

Now that you have all the necessary information about the various tools and materials needed for watercolors you are ready to start painting.

But before you set out to paint from life, in order to help you, I would suggest that you look at some of the works and techniques of the great artists of the past, from Turner and Cézanne to Klee and Stolba.

Let us analyze a composition by Cézanne. A superficial glance would lead us to suppose that the artist had casually copied the fruit as it lay on the plate. But that is not the case. Cézanne studied every item in detail and placed every element so that it might be recorded on paper in the best possible way.

Observe the following points:

* the lightest part of the composition occupies exactly two thirds of the page and jumps to the forefront;
* the darkest part occupies only one third of the surface;
* the horizon line in the composition is the edge of the table;
* the dark drapery is obtained by many vertical tones that contribute to the optical illusion of depth;
* a long horizontal line and a certain number of vertical lines create the rhythm of the composition;
* the axis of the glass contributes to the vertical rhythms;
* the longer axis of the plate, seen from the front, forms a horizontal rhythm interrupted by the apple on the right near the glass;
* the composition of the fruit on the plate has horizontal and diagonal rhythms created by the position of the apples, which are grouped within an imaginary pentagon formed by three triangles.

I have studied this marvellous composition for a long time and I have been struck by the geometrical perfection of the whole, something which you can only perceive after making this kind of analysis. When analyzing the geometrical construction in the paintings of other artists, you will be surprised to find that seeming casualness is only superficial and that the harmony of the whole emanates from the compositional ability of the artist.

Paul Cézanne (1839-1906): **Apples and Glass** *(detail), 1895/1900, 8¼ × 10½ in. (20.5 × 26.5 cm), Private collection, Paris.*

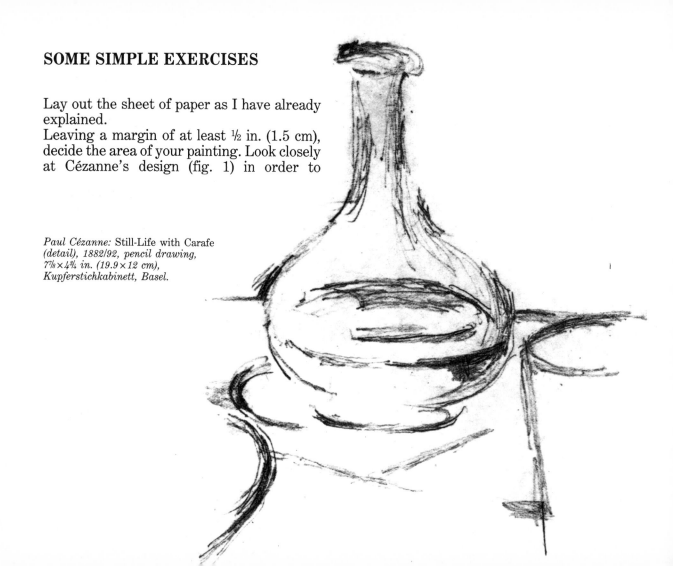

SOME SIMPLE EXERCISES

Lay out the sheet of paper as I have already explained.
Leaving a margin of at least ½ in. (1.5 cm), decide the area of your painting. Look closely at Cézanne's design (fig. 1) in order to

Paul Cézanne: Still-Life with Carafe *(detail), 1882/92, pencil drawing, 7⅞×4¾ in. (19.9×12 cm), Kupferstichkabinett, Basel.*

remember the shape. Draw an apple, trying to imitate Cézanne's (fig. 2).

2

You should normally keep at hand some soft hair brushes (sable or pole cat) No. 2 and No. 5. You will find, in fact, that after a little practice two brushes are quite enough for a painting. The different brush strokes are created by the different ways you use the brush.

For this exercise in particular you will need a round brush of soft hair (sable or pole cat) No. 5. With this brush you can draw thin and broad strokes with great ease according to how you manipulate it — either flat, or upright using the tip (fig. 3).

As I have already said, a watercolor painting is begun with the lightest color, and, as each layer dries, darker colors are superimposed with the tip of the brush barely stained with paint diluted to the transparency of a rosé wine.

3

Stage 1: First, brush in the background using a straw color obtained by mixing Cadmium Yellow, Burnt Sienna and Emerald Green in the quantities indicated next to the drawing (fig. 4). Test the color on a piece of paper, the same as the one you will use for your painting and compare your result to Cézanne's.

If the paint is too green, little by little add some yellow and Burnt Sienna.
If it is too red, add some yellow only.
If it is too yellow, add a little of the other two colors.
To obtain the straw-colored background you can also mix small amounts of other colors, such as Raw Sienna, Raw Umber, Burnt Umber, and a lot of Cadmium Yellow.
Stage 2: For the shadowed part of the apple prepare an orange tint by mixing a lot of Vermilion and very little Ultramarine Blue and compare it, as I have already explained, with Cézanne's color.
Always use plenty of water with the paint.

When the color has dried on the paper and the paper is again taut, go over it with the same color, using a firm and continuous stroke (as if you were peeling an apple with a penknife) without going back, otherwise the colors underneath will stain (fig. 5).

5

If you want to create a different effect, go over the original color with a new one while the first one is still wet. When the two colors dry they will fuse and won't be seen as super-imposed (fig. 6).

6

If you want to obtain a blotted effect, let a drop of the new color fall on top of the previous one and work it delicately with the tip of the brush (fig. 7).

7

Stage 3: Paint the shadows by mixing a lot of Ultramarine Blue with just a small drop of Carmine.

Dilute the resulting purple and try the effect on your piece of spare paper: if the color is too red add more blue; if it is too blue add some red. When the color is perfectly dry mark the edges with a little Cadmium Yellow on the purple.

Observe the two shadows and compare their colors. The darker one is the colder, that is, the one with more blue, while the lighter one has more red (fig. 8).

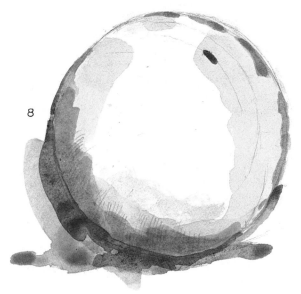

8

If you want it as dark as possible add a little Cadmium Yellow to the Ultramarine Blue plus Carmine.
If the three colors are mixed in equal proportions you will get a genuine painter's black, or Bistre (fig. 9). When diluted to varying degrees, Bistre will give you shades of gray quite different from those obtained by using black, which produces a dull and heavy effect.

9

In carrying out these exercises you will have learned to mix the colors. You will also have learned that you can create a watercolor by superimposing washes of color after the initial color has dried, and that colors can be superimposed when the original is still wet or when it is just damp.
These techniques are generally used at the same time. Most watercolorists who produce very fresh and dynamic paintings use all these techniques in their work, covering or leaving just a trace of the original pencil marks. The following exercise is designed to give you further practice:
* Draw a long, narrow rectangle and divide it into seven equal parts to make boxes.

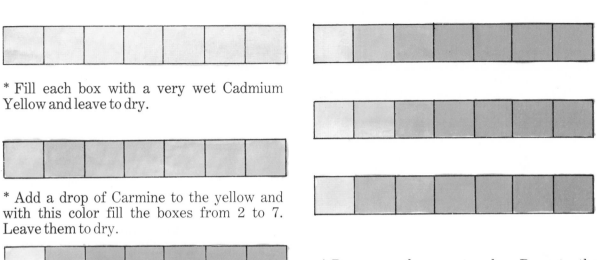

* Fill each box with a very wet Cadmium Yellow and leave to dry.

* Add a drop of Carmine to the yellow and with this color fill the boxes from 2 to 7. Leave them to dry.

* Add more red to this last color and fill the boxes 3 to 7.

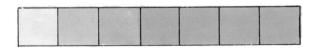

* Continue in this way, adding a little more Carmine each time. The seventh box will be orange.

* Draw another rectangle. Repeat the experiment this time using Carmine plus Ultramarine Blue.

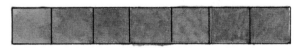

* Repeat the exercise using Ultramarine Blue and Cadmium Yellow.

* Repeat the exercise, this time with Carmine as the base and superimposing Emerald Green. You will get Bistre.

Base	Superimposition
Raw Sienna	+ Vermilion Red
» »	+ Emerald Green
» »	+ Cadmium Yellow
» »	+ Ultramarine Blue
» »	+ Carmine
» »	+ Raw Umber
» »	+ Burnt Umber
» »	+ Burnt Sienna

Working with each color in turn as a base, repeat the exercise superimposing all the other colors. I started with Raw Sienna and superimposed Vermilion. Then, still using Raw Sienna as the base, I added first Emerald Green and then each of the other colors. I then repeated the exercise using Vermilion as the base and adding Raw Sienna, then Emerald Green, and so on.

This is a very useful exercise, though it may seem long and boring, and one which is worth doing with care and precision.

A simple exercise

Let us start with a simple pencil drawing and then paint it.

You will need some good quality rough paper (50 per cent cotton fiber, if possible) which you have already stretched. To identify the correct side to use, hold the paper against the light and find the watermark. The right side of the paper is the one on which the watermark is the right way round for reading. Note the difference in the grain of the paper on the two sides. Once you have learned to recognize the right side of the paper by the grain you won't have to hunt for the watermark.

Pin the paper to a board so that it is taut. Now, using a sharpened, soft pencil, do a small drawing (about the size of a safety-match box).

Try, for instance, copying some simple shape, such as a few sage leaves and a small branch of rosemary (fig. 1).

Arranging the composition

Try to make your composition appear natural and casual even though you have arranged it with great care. (Think of music: the notes seem to follow each other naturally and spontaneously, yet they are the result of long study and great thought.)

Suppose we have a rectangular sheet of paper, three sage leaves and a sprig of rosemary. We must arrange the leaves and

If the axis of one leaf is vertical (fig. 2) it must be matched by a horizontal axis (fig. 3).

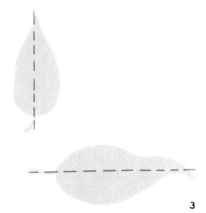

the sprig so that they make a harmonious composition and create a balance with the space around them (fig. 1).

Likewise, if one axis is slanted it must be matched by another axis slanting the other way (fig. 4).

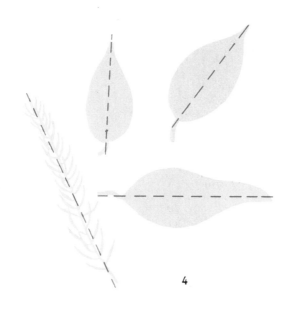

4

Adding color

Use a soft No. 3 brush. To obtain a light green for the base, mix Emerald Green, Ultramarine Blue and Carmine in the quantities indicated below:

Remember to try out the color on a separate piece of paper of the same type that you are using for your watercolor. If the color is too cold add a little red. If it is too warm add a very small amount of blue. If it is too purple add a little yellow.

After you have painted in the ground color, continue by painting each area of color, remembering to start with the darkest areas, following these tones:

Look closely at the darkest part of the sage leaf. To obtain this shade you must use a greater quantity of blue than that used for the base color.

These are suggestions, not rules, of course. You will learn much about composition from studying the postcard reproductions you can buy of the works of great artists which are always composed within an ideal geometric figure. Put a piece of tracing paper over each picture and using a ruler draw the lines of the imaginary geometrical figure enclosing the painting.

The green of the rosemary is much warmer and is composed of Emerald Green, Cadmium Yellow, Carmine, and Ultramarine Blue.

The color of the stalk is made up of Raw Sienna with Raw Umber added in the proportions indicated. Look at the shadows. I have painted them in three different ways. With Raw Umber I have created a very soft and delicate shadow which barely separates the two planes and creates a very slight impression of depth. Raw Umber is used in watercolors that have a very delicate tone. The purple shadow should not be used indiscriminately: here, for instance, it is rather strident next to the sage leaf. This effect is more usually found in Expressionistic watercolors, where one color is juxtaposed to another to create a deliberately violent dissonance. The blue shadow, as you can see, is much more pleasing. In this example I have used a very pure color so that the result is obvious, but you will get a more subtle effect by adding to the blue a drop of the color you used to paint the object casting the shadow.

A small pot of flowers

I did the watercolor shown on the following page, which has been reproduced to the same size as the original, in order to introduce you to a new exercise, still working on a small scale.

Position a pot of flowers so that the light and shade are well defined. Sketch the pot and plant, and pencil in the shadows.

Now start painting as I have taught you, trying to get as close as possible to the colors of the original.

For this exercise use a No. 6 brush and prepare a palette with the colors indicated.

A medium-sized pot of flowers

To paint a medium-sized watercolor you must follow some rules that have been devised after long experience and continuous exercise.

Choose a heavy paper and draw the outline in pencil, using the same pencil for the shadows. The drawing must be perfect. Continue correcting and perfecting your drawing until you have it right.

Don't accept a poor-quality drawing because you are in a hurry to start painting. A poor and uncertain sketch will mar your painting.

Fill two large basins with clean water. (Remember, it is important to have clean water always at hand if you are to obtain pure and not dirty colors).

In one basin rinse out the brush, then rinse it again in the other basin to ensure that it is quite clean and will not dirty the next color you will use.

Sometimes in large-scale watercolors you may have to delay the drying of the paint so that the superimposed colors blend better. To do this, add three drops of glycerine to just under a pint (half a liter) of water (no more) and wet the brush with this solution.

For large-scale watercolors which require large brushes, I find it more practical to use large blocks of paint, or better still, tubes of paint. Remember that watercolors in tubes, even if dry, can be regenerated with a little water.

Arrange the colors in order from the warmest to the coldest, following the order described on pages 11-12, as I did in my watercolor of a pot of flowers, reproduced on the following page.

A large watercolor is painted with the same materials and technique as a small or medium-sized one, but you must paint it much more quickly. It is important, therefore, to look very carefully at the subject and to prepare enough color.

Remember to try out each color on the usual piece of spare paper. Leave it to dry, and if it corresponds to the color that you want apply it quickly, working in just the same way as you would with a small watercolor. Most importantly, remember that it would be a mistake to use small brushes for a large watercolor.

E. marti 1979

A watercolor by Anna Pavesi

For this book I asked the painter Anna Pavesi to paint a still-life on paper measuring 19½×27½ in. (50×70 cm). When I went to meet her to discuss the painting what struck me most was her great love of watercolors.

"Preparing oneself to paint a watercolor," she told me, "is a very joyful experience, yet, it is also the most precarious position in which a painter can find him or herself. The fear of making an irreparable mistake can compromise the result. Instead, one needs decision and determination but, at the same time, one must have maximum fluidity, capturing the liquid and holding it in check, exploiting the innumerable possibilities that one is offered."

To understand this let us look for a moment at the four phases of Anna Pavesi's watercolor (figs. 1, 2, 3, 4). You will find that what she says corresponds to her experience as a painter.

But what can one say, what advice can one give to those who approach watercolor painting for the first time with the aim of attaining results like hers? Here are some useful suggestions:

1. Before you paint make sure that everything you need is close at hand. Do not

First stage of Anna Pavesi's watercolor.

set yourself a time limit because, although painting in watercolors can give quick results, great concentration with no interruption is necessary.

2. Remember that a flower subject requires a less-detailed drawing, which must be done with just a few essential strokes to determine the position of the flowers on the page. (From this you will appreciate the importance of knowing how to draw.)

The most luminous tones are given by the white of the paper, so you should work out in advance which areas will not be touched with color. To make things easier, you can outline these areas in pencil.

In the initial application you set the base color of the flowers, and it would be wise to keep it light so that superimpositions of other colors (which you gradually add to define your subject better) will not make the painting muddy.

3. There are numerous methods of painting watercolors. I shall describe the technique of superimposed washes. Obviously with each application of color the previous one must be dry. Remember that from the first brush strokes you must feel instinctively if the result is going to be good.

In the second application you should paint

2

38

dabs of color to the edges of the flower areas which must preserve their luminosity; these dabs serve as a base for the leaves.

4. Decide if further superimpositions are necessary. But be careful — each brush stroke may enhance the character of the subject but may also spoil its beauty. Often a color is perfect at its first application. With experience you will reach that level of artistic intuition that will tell you when to stop.

5. The third phase of the coloring process further defines the shape of the flowers, emphasizing the various petals with decisive brush strokes.

In the final phase the painting is brought to life with touches and decisive strokes of color which give the watercolor its characteristic, magic appearance.

The base colors used are the following:

3

A more complex composition for a large-scale watercolor

For this subject you will need a white cup, a few eggs, a brown saucepan, some slices of bread, a white plate, and a brown-and-white checked tablecloth.

Follow the same procedure that you used to study the watercolor by Cézanne.

Arrange your still-life so that it has the same characteristics as the one reproduced on the following page. Note the rhythms produced by the oval shapes of the plate, cup, and saucepan seen in perspective. Then find the axes that are in opposition (those of the eggs and the handle of the saucepan). The whole is contained within the rhythm of the checkered drapery in the background, created by a simple tablecloth.

The colors used are the following:

Anna Pavesi's finished watercolor.

40

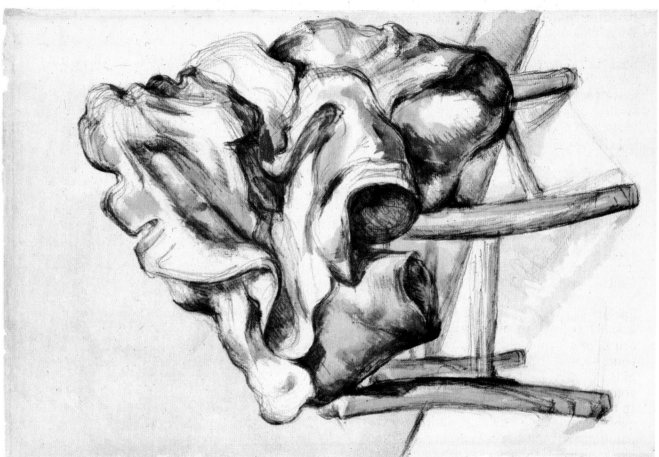

Painting fabric folds

To paint a fold of cloth one proceeds as if it were a still-life, taking into account the vertical, horizontal, and diagonal rhythms.

Copy different folds arranged in such a way as to form sharply differentiated light and shade. Cézanne's watercolor (page 42) gives us an idea of how a study of a fold can be set out. Place a sheet of tracing paper over Cézanne's work and try to retrace the artist's construction. Then lay out a fold with the same geometrical form.

Do at least one watercolor a day on this subject until you have mastered the technique.

Copy whatever strikes your fancy. Take a small box of watercolors and a water container with you wherever you go.

Learn to paint quickly and concisely. It is better to work on a small scale with a continuous line in one brush stroke. Fill in your drawing with one drop of color, pausing with the brush for a moment on the darkest area of the painting, where you need a deeper tone. The initial drop of color will spread out and make your painting come alive.

In time each watercolorist creates his or her own technique. Some combine watercolor painting with drawing in India ink, others like to sketch the outlines in sanguine or charcoal. The most rigorous artists tend to eliminate all traces of the drawing, leaving just the pure watercolors. The best painters sketch their subjects directly with the brush. I have sketched a cloth hung on a line and blown by the wind with short strokes, marking the shadows with a few dabs of color.

43

Giorgio Morandi (1890-1964): Still-Life *(detail), 1962, 12¾×9 in. (32.3×23 cm), Private collection, Milan.*

A STILL-LIFE BY GIORGIO MORANDI

Morandi painted many watercolors, some with only one color (see opposite). As you can see, this watercolor is painted in a very spare, simple style: an uninterrupted pencil line, a shadow area painted with Burnt Umber on rough and damp paper.

To paint a watercolor in this style:

* place a few glasses and bottles in a row against a white background (this is to eliminate the translucent effect of the glass);
* look at the object with your eyes half open to obtain an immediate visual synthesis, very similar to an out-of-focus photograph;
* select a horizontal composition with the light coming in from one side only;
* look very carefully at the composition, memorize it, then, without looking at it, draw what you remember, almost without taking the pencil off the sheet (fig. 1);
* wet the paper with a bristle brush. With a sable-hair brush and some Burnt Umber, paint the shadow areas only. The damp paper will give you the particular effect you are after (fig. 2).

FLOWERS BY EMIL NOLDE

Emil Nolde (1867-1956): Summer Flowers, *undated, 11⅝×16¾ in. (29.5×42.7 cm), Sprengel Museum, Hanover.*

Emil Nolde, like many other Expressionist painters, used watercolors because of the great potential of this medium to create vibrating color effects. For the tormented poetic inspiration of the Expressionist painters this was the ideal way to blend and superimpose the tones and color shades.

This particular watercolor technique is generally used for large-scale works, and to understand it fully you have to look at Nolde's picture with half-closed eyes as for the water-color by Morandi. You will then see that the flower composition is not contained within the frame but spills out of it on all sides.

Arrange a composition of flowers in which warm colors dominate. Don't bother to stretch the paper because in Expressionist painting the marks produced by the paper's buckling have value and significance.

Drawing as you did for the preceding exercise, outlining only the essentials, copy Nolde's design.

Prepare a palette with Carmine, Vermilion, Cadmium Yellow, Emerald Green, Ultramarine Blue, and Burnt Sienna (fig. 1). Dilute the Burnt Sienna and use it as a background wash. Follow the sequence from fig. 2 to fig. 4.

This exercise, carried out in the size of the

1

2

3

4

Painting abstracts in watercolor

In abstract painting, watercolors have been used by artists to explore the boundaries between the possible and the impossible, reality and unreality, order and chaos.

Color can be applied not only with a brush but with many other implements, such as sponges, feathers, or the fingers; it can be sprayed, glued, splashed, or dripped. In short, all ways of applying color are valid, indeed almost indispensable in abstract painting.

Great abstract painters have used some surprising techniques, and to express their ideas have even used substances that repel watercolors, or paper prepared with linseed oil or chalk. Klee, Kandinsky, Stolba, the Delaunays and Malevich, among others, have given to this style of painting an impetus similar to that given to watercolors by Cézanne in the nineteenth century. Abstract watercolor painting started from scratch and created its own techniques.

For this reason the abstract artist, besides having a great command of theory, must also be a first-class figurative artist and have a profound understanding of the colors, implements, and materials he is to use. Only then can he abandon pure figurative painting and enter into the inner world of abstraction.

example reproduced here, on damp paper and with a large brush, will force you to develop a conciseness which, after a certain number of exercises, you will be able to apply to large-scale watercolors. When painting large-scale works try flat sable-hair brushes: they will force you into even greater conciseness. Try also working on rough and light paper. It is always useful, too, to make a small study and then reproduce it on a larger scale. Repeat the same color blots as the study, without going into detail or getting too fussy; the permeation and fusion of the colors will substitute any detail or prettiness.

ABSTRACT DESIGNS BY LEOPOLD STOLBA

Look at the first of Stolba's two watercolors (reproduced on the following pages) of a series of differently colored concentric circles. It is difficult to tell exactly how Stolba obtained this particular effect, but I can show you how to obtain effects very similar to his.

The choice of paper is very important. It must have a special grain, such as that of Canson paper, and be of a light gray color.

Begin the exercise by mixing Carmine and Emerald Green to get Bistre. When the color is right, wet the brush and let a drop of paint fall on the sheet. Rinse the brush and rub it on to a cake of plain soap; add water and let a drop of the soapy solution fall on the center (fig. a). The soap and water will repel the color. Now apply to the center a drop of white watercolor (fig. b). When the paint is almost dry, make a small red circle with the brush (fig. c).

Continue in this way and you will achieve effects remarkably similar to those of Stolba.

These experiments will help you to explore the possibilities of watercolors and achieve the particular effects you want.

Observe the effects produced when certain liquids come into contact with others. Note, for example, what happens when you spray some oil paint heavily diluted with oil of turpentine on to a very wet watercolor. Try also spraying ordinary pencil fixative on to a wash of well-diluted watercolor.

Carry out your experiments on small pieces of heavy paper and record not only the materials you use (paper, color, brushes, etc.) but also how you applied them, how much you diluted the colors, and wetted the paper, etc.

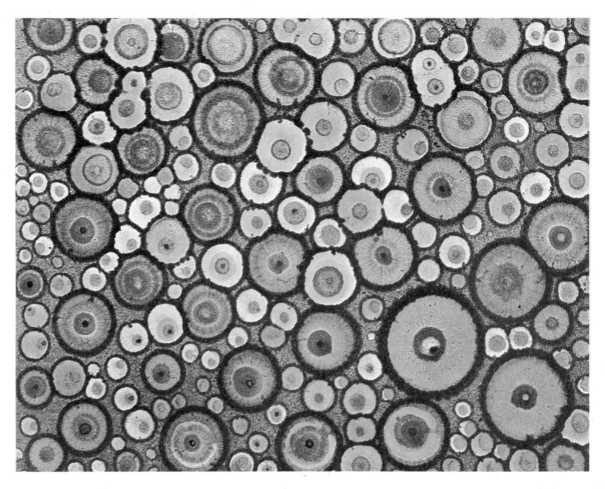

Leopold Stolba (1863-1929): Abstract Decoration, *8¼×6½ in. (21×16.5 cm), Kupferstichkabinett der Akademie der Bildenden Künste, Vienn*

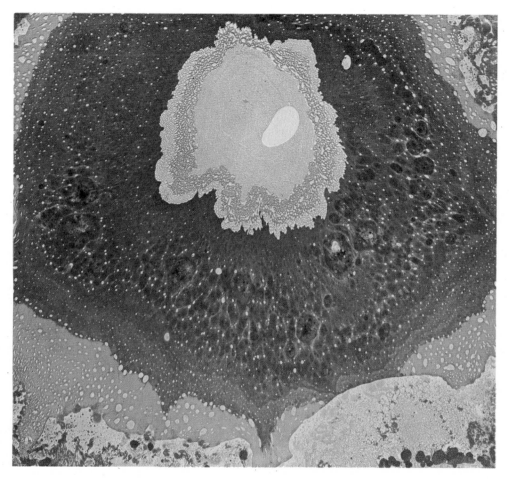

Leopold Stolba: Abstract Decoration, *11¼ × 6¼ in. (28.2 × 15.8 cm), Kupferstichkabinett der Akademie der Bildenden Künste, Vienna.*

Stolba's second watercolor suggests a substance similar to marble.

To experiment in this technique we have to start from a very simple base. On a highly diluted light background let fall a drop of well-diluted Burnt Umber. Using the handle of the brush, work the paint to the appearance of marble (fig. 1). Now try preparing a ground with plain soap and, without letting it dry, apply the heavily diluted color very quickly; you will get an effect very similar to that in fig. 2. If you mix the two substances you get a third result (fig. 3).

On to a background thus prepared drop a tiny quantity of soapy water, then immediately add

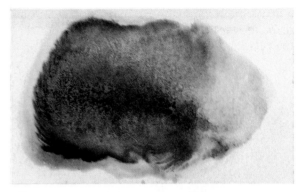

2

3

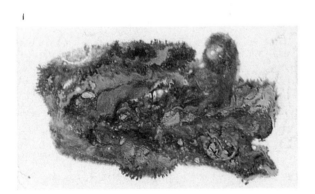

a drop of Ultramarine Blue; the result will be different again (fig. 4). If you continue this exercise on the same sheet of paper, adding drops of soapy water and new colors as you have done so far, you will achieve some really extraordinary effects (fig. 5).

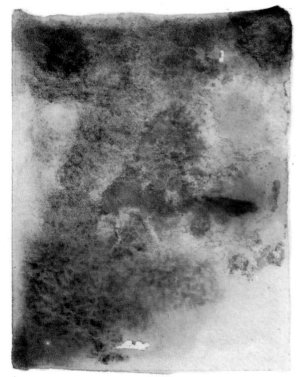

4

5

Now you should try another experiment.
Dilute some Vermilion on a plate. Wet some steel wool and rub it on to a cake of plain soap until it is full of lather.

Now dab the steel wool on to the Vermilion you have prepared on the plate until the lather and color are completely mixed. Apply the colored foam to the paper by dabbing it with the steel wool (fig. 6).

If you want a more concentrated background repeat the application (fig. 7).

If you want a background with more color, intensify the base color (fig. 8).

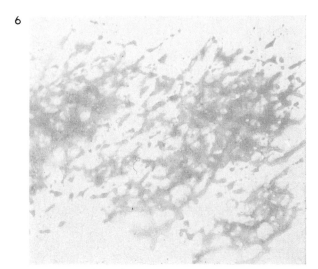

You can obtain a marble-grained background by adding different drops of different colors to the background while it is still wet (fig. 9).

9

Experimenting with new materials in abstract painting is not the only way in which these painters used watercolors. Paul Klee found in traditional watercolor the most suitable way of expressing his ideas of the world of form, figuration and color, by painting on paper or canvas prepared with chalk or clay.

Preparation of a canvas for water-color painting

Soak some tablets of animal glue in cold water in the proportions 1 to 12; double boil and then take off the heat. Before the solution cools down add some Kaolin chalk, mixing continuously so as not to let lumps form. When you have a mixture the density of yoghurt, measure out two spoonfuls of hot linseed oil for every cup of solution, (which should be still warm) and mix. Apply evenly to a taut canvas with a wide flat brush.

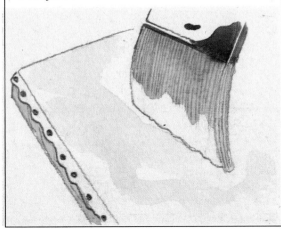

DAY AND NIGHT IN THE WORKS OF PAUL KLEE

Before going on to analyze a watercolor by Klee, it will help to say something about his attitude to painting. In fact, in Klee's work, theory and practice interact so closely that even in a practical manual it is impossible to ignore the theory.

Klee thought that every element in nature was richer in color than any painter's palette. Therefore the artist does not paint nature; rather, he paints *from* nature. To avoid this dead end Klee didn't look at painting as such but at its possibilities for growth and reproduction, exactly as a seed germinates and grows into a plant.

Form is not an end in itself but is in continual evolution, and color is the key to the magical world of the imagination. The world has two sides to it, life and death, day and night, black and white. Each color has its complementary color which contrasts with and integrates it. To darken red you need green; to make violet warmer a drop of yellow must be added.

The artist's intention should be to reconstruct poetically the texture of the universe, transforming it at his pleasure whenever he chooses, changing it perhaps by a small drop of color with the power of a primitive king in his magical forest.

Klee passes on from the discovery of light (and therefore of color) as a modelling and liberating element, to the consideration of geometry and compositional materials. In his paintings he blends line, color and form to achieve a unique and mysterious atmosphere. Color is not a logical sequence of tones, but an above-below, backwards-forwards, right-left rhythm facing the artist, whose task it is to balance such elements. Time and space are colors that never stop; what was to the left is now to the right, what came first now comes after. Also, what you are coloring is by no means certain: it may be there or it may not. While one is painting everything is transformed: the sketch is no longer a firm starting point but a seed from which infinite paintings, of infinite sizes and colors can grow. We can call this process an endless metamorphosis of quantity and quality.

Now try to apply the thinking of Klee, taking as inspiration the following exercise from his book, *Theory of Form and Figuration*.

Paul Klee (1879-1940): Flowers on the Sand, *9¼×11¾ in. (23.5×30.5 cm), Felix Klee collection, Berne.*

Draw a square 8 × 8 in. (20 × 20 cm) and divide each side into ten parts. Join the points opposite each other, making 100 small squares representing 50 days and 50 nights (fig. 1).

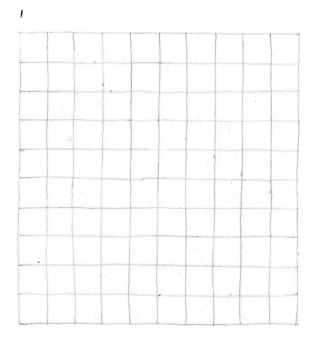

Some nights are darker than others, while the days are much the same. Days and nights go by without anything unusual happening, without any changes (or at least so it seems to us) (fig. 2).

58

3

4

But then we meet a person we like and see him or her for three warm days. When the person leaves we are despondent. Now and then, at night, we think about our friend: thus we have cold nights (fig. 3).

Spring arrives, the days get longer, the weather gets warmer, the nights are less dark. The earth is bustling with life, buds break through, the sun warms the earth by day. Color takes over (fig. 4).

PAINTING FIGURES

In this chapter dedicated to the figure, I shall show how to sketch a static figure and a moving one, how to do a full-length portrait and a bust, and how to deal with anatomical details and the drawing of animals.

Up to this point you have worked solely on inanimate objects to which you give life by the use of color. Now you will be working from life, and will therefore have to grasp life even in its most modest expressions, represent it, and extol it.

The techniques remain unchanged, both in small-scale and large-scale paintings, but you will need to work more quickly. Figure-painting in watercolors particularly needs immediacy.

Let us begin by analyzing and copying some sketches and studies of such great masters as Van Gogh and Delacroix who, as we shall discover, anticipated modern painting. Often we will find written inscription on these studies, which suggests that the artists used to keep these notebooks or sketchbooks in their pocket together with their colors, brushes, and flasks of water.

You too can easily supply yourselves with the necessary materials and equipment.

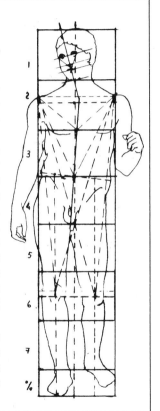

Structure of the human figure

Since the time of Vitruvius the proportions of the human body have been seen in multiples and submultiples of the head. The ideal human figure is traditionally based on very precise proportions: the whole body is seven and a half times longer than the head, the shoulders are twice as broad as the head, the neck is half as long as the head, and so on for all the parts of the body, as shown in the diagram. Once this rule is understood we can begin to study the human figure.

A WATERCOLOR BY IPPOLITO CAFFI

Ippolito Caffi (1809-1866): Popular Venetian Types, *1848/49, Museo del Risorgimento, Venice.*

Ippolito Caffi, a painter and watercolorist, began by painting views in which his use of light recalls the works of Canaletto. An adventurous man, he made several journeys to the East and came back with many sketches and paintings. He also took part in the movements advocating Italy's independence and painted battle scenes from life.

His watercolor reproduced here is an ideal aid to our understanding of how to begin making small studies of figures.

Here we see all the stages for the painting of figures: in the lower half of the sheet are a number of figures sketched in sepia, as was the custom in the nineteenth century; in the top left-hand corner three figures with well-defined shadows have been drawn; as we move further to the right the figures are defined in more detail.

Painting a watercolor in the style of Caffi

Now we have established a starting point for the first figure study.

With a 2B pencil draw the outline of a figure, without any shadows, roughly the same size as those in figs. 1 and 2. Now, as Caffi did, apply a background of a dullish color, cover-

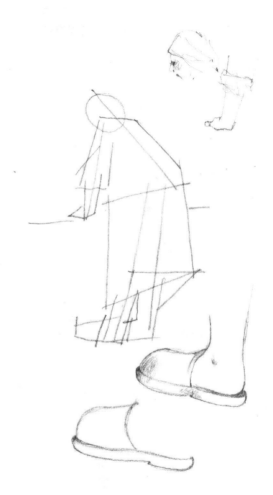

ing only the shadow areas (fig. 3). This color can be obtained by mixing Ultramarine Blue and Vandyke Brown and adding a touch of Cadmium Yellow if the color seems too cold; the color should be strongly diluted.

The final stage (fig. 4) is painted with the following colors. For the complexion, use a mixture of Raw Sienna and well diluted Vermilion. Once this color is dry, wash with Raw Umber in the darker areas. For the scarf use Burnt Umber with a drop of Raw Umber. For the lighter areas of the jacket use Burnt Umber, for the half-tones in the jacket Raw Umber, and for the darker areas Ultramarine Blue.

These areas must be painted while the colors are still wet on the paper. Before the paint dries completely, apply a drop of Ultramarine Blue and a little Carmine to the darker areas — you will get a rather special effect.

By mixing Emerald Green with Carmine and Vandyke Brown you will get the dark color you need for the skirt; where the black is warmest you will have to add more red. In the darker areas of the skirt add Ultramarine Blue to give it more depth. As the stockings are of a darker color use a thicker mix of equal parts of red and green. For the clogs use the same as for the stockings but more diluted.

You will have noticed that I have not put the scale of colors next to the painting. This is because your subject will not require the

2

same range of colors as the example, and because by now you should have a certain command of colors. For your first few attempts select simple subjects such as peasant women wearing plain long skirts or an old man well muffled up. As you become more proficient you can pass on to more difficult subjects, such as the ones I will suggest.

3

4

A DUTCH GIRL BY VINCENT VAN GOGH

Talking of peasants I am immediately reminded of Van Gogh. The following letter will help you to appreciate the torment and anguish of this painter. It is a letter he wrote to his brother Théo, in which, among other things, he mentions the watercolor reproduced on the next page.

"Dear Théo,
Perhaps you are waiting for news of what I'm up to now. I'm also waiting for your news. I still go to Mauve [a cousin of Van Gogh's and also a painter] every day. In the mornings and afternoons I paint and in the evenings I draw. Up to now I have done five studies and two watercolors and, of course, some sketches. I can't tell you how kind Mauve and Jet have been to me at this time.
Mauve has taught me many things which, naturally, I can't get right straight away but after a lot of practice I will. Therefore I must work very hard and when I return to Etten I shall have to make some changes. Among other things I have to rent somewhere a room large enough so that I can work at a sufficient distance from my subjects; otherwise it is impossible to draw a figure, let alone the details.
I intend to ask Mauve's advice about this and soon I will be able to tell you something more definite. The oil paintings that I've done are still-life studies, while for the watercolors I used a girl from Scheveningen as a model.
Perhaps Mauve will write to you before long. However, I've been here almost a month now and, as you can imagine, I've had a lot of expenses.
Although it's true that Mauve has given me several things (paints, etc.), I've had to buy many things and I even paid the model for a few days.
Besides, I needed a new pair of shoes and, to be honest, I spent too much on them. I have thus spent more than 200 Fr. Apart from that, everything included, the journey cost me 90 schillings.
Now it seems that father is rather broke and I don't know what to do. Personally I would still like to stay here and rent a room in Scheveningen for a few months (perhaps longer), but considering my financial position I think it is best if I return to Etten.

Scheveningen is a wonderful place, full of typical characters.

But models are very expensive, 1.50 or 2 schillings a day and even more.

Naturally I have the advantage of being in close contact with painters, etc.

I have written to father to ask him for more money but he will scold me for having spent more than 90 schillings. I think you will understand that it is not a huge sum, for everything is very expensive. But I do not like having to account for every penny I spend, especially as he then goes and tells everybody and exaggerates in the process.

So I have to confess to you that I am rather broke, and that is why I'm writing to you. I don't have enough money to stay or to come back to Etten.

However, I'll wait here for a few days and do what you advise. Don't you think it's better that I stay here a little longer? I would be very happy and I wouldn't return home before I had made some progress.

If instead you want me to return immediately I shall do so, but then I'll have to find a good room somewhere, larger than the small studio I have at the moment. That way I could work better and return to The Hague in a while.

Vincent Van Gogh (1853-1890): Girl from Scheveningen.

Whatever you decide, thanks to Mauve I have begun to understand the mysteries of paints and watercolors.

And that is my repayment for the 90 schillings I spent on the journey.

Mauve says my star is rising but is still hidden behind the clouds. It's a challenge that spurs me on. One day I'll tell you in detail exactly how good and understanding Mauve has been to me.

Anyway, I'll wait a few days for your answer. If I don't hear from you in three or four days I'll ask father for the money to return home immediately.

I have many things to tell you which will probably interest you about the system they have at Etten of drawing from models, but I'll write in detail some other time.

I enclose some small sketches of the two watercolors. I am confident that before long I can produce something that I can sell and, if necessary, I could find a buyer even for these watercolors, especially the one Mauve retouched a little. But I would rather keep them for a while so that I can be reminded of certain aspects of their composition.

What a wonderful medium to render atmosphere and distance! The figure seems to breathe the air that surrounds it! Would you like me to make you another series of watercolors while I'm here? I couldn't ask for more, only board and lodging, models, paints, paper etc. Everything costs money and I don't have any. So, whatever you think, please let me know by return of post and, if you want me to stay send me, if possible, some money. Having already learned so much about colors and how to use a brush I think I would make more rapid progress. And I hope to do so, so that Mauve never regrets the kindness that she has shown me. I'm going to be successful no matter what happens. Good-bye for now,

yours, Vincent"

Painting a watercolor
in the style of Van Gogh

If we look at the watercolor as a whole we notice that the painting is based on earth colors. In fact each color used by the artist, including the white bonnet, contains a small percentage of the base color. If you look at it with your eyes half-closed you will notice that most of the light, which comes from above, falls on to the bonnet and the arms.

Ask someone to be your model, dressed more

or less like the girl in Van Gogh's painting.

Remember that the figure you are going to paint should be at a distance from you of at least three times her height, otherwise you won't be able to take it all in with one glance. Remember too that the smaller the water-color, the further from you the figure should be.

Sketch the figure as in the preceding exercise, then start painting the wall in the background. The base color in the example (page 69) is formed from Ultramarine Blue and Burnt Umber. As you can see, the background is not uniform; I have accentuated the warm parts by adding Burnt Sienna and in the cold areas I have added Ultramarine Blue.

The different colors should be superimposed while they are still wet. Let the drops fall one by one and work them delicately with the brush.

The colors adapt themselves to the grain of the paper as they dry, producing those effects so characteristic of watercolors.

Look at the example again with half-closed eyes and note that the darkest part of the background has the same visual weight as the dark areas of the figure, while the light floor space has the same weight as the lighter

areas of the figure.

Now let's take a close look at the scarf which has been painted in by a very diluted Bistre. The face, neck, and arms have been painted in Burnt Umber and Vermilion.

For the first shadow area use a rather diluted color to begin with and then strengthen it with a little Burnt Umber. Adding yet more Burnt Umber, paint the second area of shadow.

Next, apply color to the cheek only, adding a very little Vermilion to make the tone of the face even warmer.

The neck area, where the color is colder, should be painted by adding Ultramarine Blue to the color you used for the second area of shadow.

Mix Ultramarine Blue and Raw Umber with a touch of Carmine to get the blue tone of the dress.

For the stockings and slippers add Vandyke Brown to the color used for the dress.

If, as you work, you notice that the background is too light compared with the dress, retouch it — and again if necessary — until you get the depth you want.

To achieve a sense of transparency in the background, leave some lighter patches to stand out, as I did in my painting.

Visual weight

To check the visual weight of a mass of color, draw a series of squares each containing another square; start with a black square on a white background and vice versa, and then

use all the other colors. Note how the white square seems bigger than the black square.

This shows that a light mass of color gives the optical illusion of being bigger when compared with a dark mass of the same dimensions. Thus in a painting, the dark areas must occupy more space than the light colors to achieve a balance. As you repeat this exercise, using different colors, you can test for yourself all the possible visual weights of different colors. You will notice that the cold colors tend to shrink, while the warm ones tend to expand.

STUDIES OF A VOYAGE BY EUGENE DELACROIX

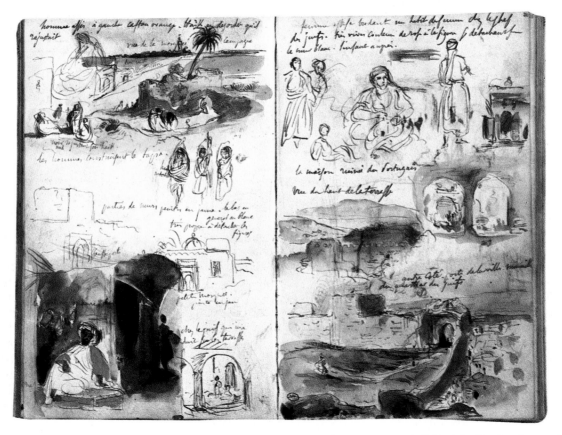

E. Delacroix (1798-1863): Pages from Moroccan Sketchbook, 7⅝ × 4⅞ in. (19.3 × 12.7 cm), *Cabinet des Dessins, Louvre, Paris.*

These "Studies of a Voyage" provide us with an incentive to draw. They are, in fact, quick, concise sketches of someone who loves to draw and who wishes to remember the voyage, quickly noting places, occurrences, and emotions.

From his journey to Spain and Morocco in 1832, Delacroix brought back seven albums of pen and watercolor sketches, each one executed with a fresh, quick and sure hand. The annotations are diverse: he noticed everything and sketched with masterly precision everything he observed.

Among his drawings are notes and jottings which were of great importance to his future development as a painter.

For Delacroix this journey meant the discovery of color: the greens of the valleys and the palm trees, the blue of distant mountains and sky, the red of a turban, or the yellow of a sand dune. His watercolor studies are full of light. Each drop of color is in correct proportion; there is nothing superfluous or ill-balanced, even though the brush strokes seem distracted and indifferent.

Nothing could be more lacking in detail, yet nothing is more detailed than these sketches. With a few strokes and some drops of color Delacroix manages to give a sense of completeness. The results of his researches into light, evident in these watercolors, would be adopted by the Impressionists fifty years later.

Let's analyze how Delacroix succeeds in balancing even a small-scale sketch, *The Arab Women*, which he made simply to record some impressions.

Remembering what you have learned about the visual weight of colors, look at the largest figure on the left and relate the space it occupies to the area at the bottom of the painting that is empty. You will see that the spaces are perfectly balanced and have opposing axes (see pages 31-32).

Now look at the central figures: they are opposed to each other; they are painted in the same colors, with the same amount of white, and if we prolong their axes they will cross. The incomplete figure in the top right-hand corner counterbalances the void under the seated figures.

This sense of equilibrium which we have discovered in the sketch was, to a painter like Delacroix, as natural and instinctive as breathing and eating. You too, with continued application and study, can achieve this sense.

Eugène Delacroix: Studies of Arab Women, *6¼ × 8⅜ in. (15.8 × 21.3 cm), Cabinet des Dessins, Louvre, Paris.*

Travelling with a sketchbook

All you need is a sketchbook, a small box of watercolors, a knapsack on your back and the desire to go out and paint.

If you are lucky you will start out for the East; if you aren't, you will find what you are looking for right behind your house, if you know how to look. In fact, there must be many people who have travelled the world and, it would seem, haven't even crossed the threshold of their own house, while there are others, gifted with the power of observation, who can find treasure in everything around them.

Learn to look at the world around you and you will find subjects to paint right under your nose, and sun and light without limits.

Draw a figure with one continuous motion, just the outline. It isn't easy and a lot of practice is needed.

Start by copying people when they are sitting down (they are likely to stay in the same position for longer); then when you are confident enough, try drawing moving figures.

To learn to sketch a figure you must learn to observe the subject for a long time, trying to memorize as much as possible of what you see. Then, with one stroke of the pencil (use the same technique as for the exercise on page 45), draw as much as you can remember.

Then look back at the subject and correct whatever seems wrong to you without erasing anything. If there is a mistake in an area that will be painted, it will be hidden by the paint. If the mistake is outside this area don't rub it out. Once you have painted the rest it will lose importance and your design will have greater freshness.

The next study I suggest is a railway worker in various postures. All the colors are derived from the same base color, without superimpositions and without any big blobs of color. I have reinforced only the areas of dark shadows, letting the paint drip and pausing there for a moment with the brush.

To obtain the worker's jacket, I mixed Ultramarine Blue with a little Raw Umber. For the peak of his cap I used the same color but slightly thicker. For the shirt and shoes I used a thick Bistre, and for the trousers I used Cerulean Blue mixed with a drop of Bistre.

For the skin tone, which in this case has to be painted with just one application and must therefore be more rosy, I mixed some Raw Sienna with a little Carmine. A mixture of Bistre with Burnt Umber gave me the right color for his hair.

74

FROM "NOA-NOA" BY GAUGUIN

If we multiply by a hundred everything I said about Delacroix we have the light of Gauguin. Though it was in Brittany that Gauguin discovered his vocation, it was at Tahiti that his genius unfolded in his Polynesian works, with all their spontaneous primitivity.

Gauguin's research, experiments, aspirations, and the profound impressions that he gained through contacting a "barbarous" civilization were transcribed by the artist into a famous manuscript, *Noa-Noa,* edited with C. Morice, a writer and friend, in the winter of 1893-94, and illustrated with watercolors, drawings, prints, and other documents.

In 1891, in order to find his ideal light, Gauguin landed on the island of Morea. In his travel notes he wrote: "I have begun to work. But the landscape's fresh and glowing colors dazzle me... Yet it is all so simple: to paint as I see; to transpose on to a canvas a blue, a red, without artifice! The golden rivers enchant me: how long shall I hesitate before I submerge myself in all this light, this sun-filled delight?"

Speaking of the figure, he continues: "I start sketching a portrait — it is that ambiguous smile I wish to render. Annoyed, she makes an unpleasant face, says 'Aita' (No) and leaves. An hour later she comes back dressed in a beautiful skirt and with a flower behind her ear. What has happened and why has she returned? Is she flirting... or is it just a whim, so common in them? I realize that as a painter I must concern myself with the inner life of a model; a tacit and pressing urgency, almost physical possession for a decisive result..."

"I work in a hurry and with passion. I put into this portrait what the mind allows the eye to see, and, above all, that which the eyes alone cannot see, this intimate fire, intense.... Her elevated, noble forehead brings to mind Poe's statement: 'There is no such thing as pure beauty without there being something strange in the proportions'. And the flower that she wears echoes her perfume..."

Gauguin's watercolors clearly demonstrate his conquest of a completely new and strange world in which color has become a medium of expression above all others.

Paul Gauguin (1848-1903): Four Tahitian Women, *from the* Noa-Noa *manuscript, 1893/4, 11×11¾ in. (28×30 cm), Cabinet des Dessins, Louvre, Paris*

Tahiti just round the corner

When you look at Gauguin's work, all you see is light and color. Each painted figure is full of light, every piece of clothing is imbued with color.

To find similar subjects today is not easy, but in Italy one may still be lucky enough to come across a caravan of gypsies. The gypsy girl I have painted here, moving away from the campsite to hang up some washing, has all the necessary characteristics: strong features and colorful clothes; also, she moved sufficiently slowly to allow me to copy her. You should copy your subject quickly with a very soft pencil, or, if you are skilful enough, directly with the brush. For a sketch like this use a rough, straw-colored paper if possible. The watercolor paint should be very diluted and transparent; this time apply it with a brush that you have dried a little with some absorbent paper, so that the paint will be rubbed on rather than applied in drops.

The skirt is painted in two layers of Vermilion with a drop of Carmine. The first layer must dry before the second is applied. For the first layer of her skin use Raw Sienna and a drop of Vermilion; for the second layer add some Burnt Umber.

The background is colored by various shades

of violet, obtained by mixing Ultramarine Blue and Carmine in different proportions: more red if the violet turns out too warm, more blue if it looks too cold.

Further exercises on the figure

I am now going to suggest a series of exercises reproduced here in the same size as the originals. These watercolors are part of my sketchbook in which, from time to time, I painted figures that were inspired by poetry. Such an exercise can prove very interesting. Once, while I was drawing my wife who was sitting next to an empty chair embroidering, a few lines of a poem by Edgar Lee Masters suddenly came to my mind:

...Or you shall sit alone by your own hearth,
And suddenly the chair by you shall hold a
* guest,*
And you shall know that guest,
And read the authentic message of his eyes.

Now let's look at the range of colors we need to create the impression of a room with a fire blazing in the fireplace. We will need colors that are a little warmer than those used in the illustrations. The model's hair is obtained with Raw Sienna and a little Cadmium Yellow; the red areas with Burnt Sienna and

Vermilion, which you will only superimpose when the first base is perfectly dry; the jersey you will get with Raw Umber and a little Burnt Sienna in the warmest areas; the shadow is Ultramarine Blue and Burnt Umber. Raw Sienna and Vermilion were used for the model's complexion. The skirt was painted in Umber.

The shadows have been created in a number of ways: below the white cloth I added Ultramarine Blue, while the lower left-hand side of the dress has a light wash of Ultramarine Blue and a superimposed layer of thicker Raw Umber. For the legs, I have also used Raw Umber for the half-tones, while I got the dark shadows from Ultramarine Blue, Carmine, and Raw Umber. The chairs have been painted with Burnt Umber and Ultramarine Blue (the darker one), and for the lighter areas Burnt Umber with the addition of a little Raw Sienna has been used.

A nun embroidering

Poetry, fiction and music can evoke colored images that are different in every one of us. I will show you some of the watercolors I painted inspired by poetry. Your interpretation will be very different, but it will be *yours*.

The Gypsy Nun by Federico García Lorca:

Silence of lime and myrtle.
Wild mallows among the flowering reeds.
The nun embroiders wallflowers
on a straw-colored cloth.
In the gray chandelier fly
seven birds of the prism.
The church growls in the distance
like a bear on its back.
How well she embroiders! How daintily!
On the pale-yellow cloth
she would like to embroider
flowers of her fancy.
What a sunflower! What a magnolia
of spangles and ribbons!
What saffrons and what moons
on the altar-cloth!
Five citrons are sweetening
in the nearby kitchen.
The five nasturtiums
cut in Almeria.
Through the nun's eyes
gallop two highwaymen.
An ultimate and dormant murmur
lifts her camisole,
and as she looks towards the clouds and hills
in the desolate remoteness,
her sugar and verbena heart breaks.
Oh, what a lofty plain,
with twenty suns above!

What upstanding rivers
does her fantasy visualize!
But she proceeds with her flowers,
while in the breeze,
the vertical light plays
on the lofty checkers
of the lattice-window.

In this watercolor the base must be completely dry before the next layer is superimposed.

The dark habit of the nun is obtained with three or four layers of Bistre. Do not use black at all. The same Bistre, more diluted, is used for the shadows of the white areas.

The skin tone is still obtained by using Raw Sienna and a drop of Vermilion; for areas in shadow I added Raw Umber to the face, while the shadow on the hands is obtained by a very light layer of Bistre. The colors used for the chair are Raw Sienna and Vandyke Brown.

The pots of flowers were painted with Burnt Sienna, with a wash of Bistre for the shadows. The leaves were painted in Emerald Green with the addition of a little Cadmium Yellow, the amount of yellow increasing in the lighter green areas. The bars on the window have been painted with Bistre to which some Burnt Sienna has been added

to obtain a warmer color than that of the nun's habit. The same color, but much more diluted, has been used for the wall.

Girl picking flowers in a field

I have painted two different interpretations of the following poem by Emily Dickinson:

It's all I have to bring today —
This, and my heart beside —
This, and my heart, and all the fields —
And all the meadows wide —
Be sure you count — should I forget
Some one the sum could tell —
This, and my heart, and all the bees
Which in the clover dwell.

The choice of colors in both cases is rich in Raw Sienna, starting with the hat which is composed of Raw Sienna with a touch of Raw Umber. Raw Umber is also used for the shadows.
For the face I have used Raw Sienna and a little Vermilion; the shadow area is created with a mixture of Ultramarine Blue and Raw Umber.
I mixed Vandyke Brown and a drop of Ultramarine Blue for the hair. Cadmium Red,

82

to which I added Ultramarine Blue and Vandyke Brown, makes the color of the jacket.
For the skirt I used Raw Sienna mixed with Raw Umber; for the shadows on the skirt I used the same color as for the hair, but more diluted.
The green of the field is Emerald Green, cooled down by a little Ultramarine Blue.

SHADOWS AND REFLECTIONS IN RENOIR'S WATERCOLORS

Renoir was influenced by Courbet but even more by the Franco-Spanish painter, Diaz de la Peña, who taught his pupils an important rule: "A real painter never picks up a brush unless he has an object in front of him." Renoir followed this rule throughout his life. In this watercolor he painted what ordinary people see every day; the figure is in a normal position with an ordinary dress and hat; even the light and color are unexceptional. It is nevertheless this "normality" that makes the watercolor a masterpiece.

Look at the green of the leaves, studying the enlarged details, and try to work out how many blues, greens and yellows the artist has had to experiment with to get that "normal" green. The leaves that he has left white give that sun-filled atmosphere to the painting which was so sought after by the Impressionists who, through their painting techniques, succeeded in making even the shadows appear full of light.

The trunk of the tree has an earthy, reddish color, almost the exact complement of those greens. Even the girl's yellow hat, rosy complexion and red hair add warm colors to counterbalance the blues and greens of the leaves. Her dress has a grayish tinge, a neutral color.

Let's have a look now at the two heads and try to spot the differences. The head, as the artist ultimately decided to paint it, inclines slightly, while in the small study in the bottom right-hand corner it is completely upright. In the study, the brim of the hat is much narrower and the face is more yellow in color, reflecting the color of the hat.

In the enlarged detail of the head we can see that even in the model's face there are many variations of color. The area of the face from the mouth upwards is the coldest, while the red of her cheeks is an intermediate area and her forehead, on which her red hair falls, is the warmest area. The brim of the hat has red reflections from the girl's red hair, while the peak of her hat is of a darker pink than her complexion but colder than the brim, and thus fades into the background.

Pierre-Auguste Renoir (1841-1919): Fruit Picking *(and details), 1883/86, 18¾ × 12¼ in. (47.5 × 31 cm), Cabinet des Dessins, Louvre, Paris*

Antoine Watteau (1684-1721): Studies of Heads of Men and Women *(detail), 10⅝×16½ in. (27×42 cm), Musée du Petit Palais, Paris*

PORTRAITS

Among the many types of portrait (realistic, ideal, heroic, expressive, symbolic, psychological), we can discover two main tendencies. One attempts to fix the features of the face, interpreting what is there and picking out its particular characteristics. The other tends to pass over the individual, physical characteristics and to create an idealized image of the subject. In either case the aim is to present a likeness of the subject.

If we take a look at paintings of the past we observe how carefully the artists studied the faces of their models, establishing relationships between the various parts of the face and enlarging details. I have traced construction lines on to a study of a head by Watteau in which the head is observed from different angles. Look at the alignment of the meeting points (both vertical and horizontal): the triangle formed by the tip of the nose and the outer corners of the eyes, the alignment of the eyes and the tip of the ear, which is as high as the bridge of the nose.

For the exercise I suggest you paint a profile portrait of a girl with her head very still and her face in shadow.

Work on a small scale to start with.

Sketch the head, then begin to apply color to the face. Prepare this with Raw Sienna and Vermilion, accentuating the red on the cheeks. Once the paint is dry, superimpose a mixture of Ultramarine Blue and a little Vandyke Brown, just washing it lightly.

For the head use some Raw Umber; to color

the darkest areas add a layer of very diluted Ultramarine Blue. Use Ultramarine Blue and Carmine (a drop only) for the blouse. When all is dry, add the last touches of the deepest colors to the darkest areas.

A full-face portrait

When trying this exercise choose a very young model and paint on pale yellow paper to get an effect similar to *sinopia* in medieval frescoes. Draw the head with very delicate strokes and a few touches for the shadows. Use only basic colors, such as Ultramarine Blue and Raw Umber, for the few delicate shadows, which are all on the cold side.

You will see that I have applied the paint in large masses, subdividing the shadow areas of the face into two essential parts: the forehead with its cold color and the area round the mouth with a warmer colored shadow.

The eyes, which I have hardly outlined at all, were obtained by a further application of the same Umber as was used for the shadow under the nose and the darkest part of the mouth. For the hair I used Ultramarine Blue and Raw Umber and for the shadows on the hair, I used the same color but with less water.

A portrait painted with flat washes

Before I go on to speak of half-length portraits, I should like to suggest an exercise in flat washes that should interest you. First, observe a model very closely and try to divide both the background and the subject into imaginary geometrical areas. Then paint these areas, keeping in mind the exercise after Paul Klee (see pages 58-59).

Now let's analyze the painting reproduced here, starting with the background which has been painted in different shades of green.

From the left, we see that the first area has been painted with Emerald Green, a little Ultramarine Blue and Raw Umber, while the second area was painted with the same green plus Raw Umber superimposed on to the green as soon as it dried.

For the third area (bottom left-hand corner) the same colors as for the second area were used, but more diluted.

The light green in the fourth area is a mixture of the green used in the first area and a large quantity of heavily diluted Cadmium Yellow. The dark transparency of the green was obtained by superimposing the color used in the first area (Emerald Green, Ultramarine Blue, and Raw Umber) after the first layer had dried.

The last shade of green on the right is obtained by mixing Emerald Green, Cadmium Yellow and a drop of Raw Umber.

Turning to the hair, we note three subdivisions: the lightest area (a mixture of Burnt Umber and a little Raw Umber); the darkest area, Bistre; and the half-tone (a mixture of the colors used in the previous two areas).

Now let us examine the lightest part of the face, which I subdivided into six areas. The first area at the top, which is the lightest, was painted with Raw Sienna and a little Burnt Sienna.

For the area immediately below I used the same color plus a little Carmine.

The small square under the eye I obtained by mixing a drop of Emerald Green to the colors used for the first area.

The fourth area (bordering the second) is painted with Raw Sienna, and a little Burnt Umber.

The fifth area, towards the left, is painted with Burnt Umber plus a little Raw Sienna and a speck of Raw Umber.

For the last area (corresponding to the ear) I used Raw Umber and a drop of Burnt Umber.

All the shadowed areas in the face have been created with different shades of violet. The area bordering the light part is a cold violet, made by mixing a little Ultramarine Blue, some Carmine, and just a dash of Cadmium Yellow. The red and blue should be mixed in equal proportions while the amount of yellow must be fractional (a drop the size of a pinhead). The color must be well diluted and, once dry, must be applied again to the darkest parts.

The color of the nose is formed by adding a little Carmine to the base violet color, while the eye is painted with just one stain of Bistre.

The right-hand area of the forehead is painted with the addition of a little Raw Umber to the violet base, while the left-hand area is Raw Umber plus a little violet.

On the neck we find the two colors of the face, washed over with violet, which I made by mixing Ultramarine Blue, Carmine, and very little Cadmium Yellow to soften it. I got the darkest part of the neck by using the same violet with less water.

The jersey is based on six variations of Carmine and a little Ultramarine Blue in the following order, starting from the left: eight parts of Carmine to two of Ultramarine Blue; then the same color plus a drop of Burnt Sienna; the same color again but thicker; the next color is nine parts of red and one of

blue; the following section is painted with the same color to which I added some Raw Umber; the last color is again the same, but with more water.

The apron is painted with Emerald Green and a little Ultramarine Blue added in the right-hand section; the middle area is the same green, and for the left-hand section some Cadmium Yellow was added.

You will learn some important lessons from exercises such as this, which are fundamental to your training as a watercolorist.

You will have noticed that the color segments have been obtained by mixing the base colors with their colder or warmer, lighter or darker variants.

Always remember, when trying out these exercises, to check your colors first on a piece of paper before applying them to your painting.

Two medium-sized portraits
When you try a medium-sized watercolor you should above all aim for simplicity. Draw simple shapes with a very soft pencil (3B). Use the pencil lightly so that you leave only a very slight granular mark on the paper. Your colors should be formed from just a few tones and should be applied with quick brush strokes. Paint all the shadows first, then the details.

If, while it evolves, the sketch takes on the so-called "unfinished" look, leave it as it is. Learn to recognize when a watercolor can be considered "finished," and remember that in watercolor one stroke too few is better than one too many.

The problems posed by painting a face should be solved by establishing a scale of color tones similar to that used for the flat tone portrait we have just dealt with, but with the paint applied and superimposed while the background is still wet. Only the last touches in the darkest parts are added after the painting has dried.

The range of colors used is quite simple: a well watered-down Bistre for the shadows, Ultramarine Blue with a touch of Raw Sienna for the hair; Emerald Green and Raw Sienna for all the shadows of the face. (Before the face dries you must add a wash of the same blue of the hair to the dark area between the nose and the eyes.)

Continue with Raw Sienna and Vermilion on the lighter areas of the face. Always remember to use plenty of water with your paint. You will have time to darken the colors, but if you start with the paint too thick it is difficult to correct the tones later.

Let me remind you that in a half-length portrait the pose must always appear natural.

For the first few times at least, use as your subject someone sleeping or reading, or in some other relaxed position. In time, and with experience, you will learn to arrange your models in the poses you want.

93

"STUDY OF A CARD-PLAYER" BY CEZANNE

With the experience that you have gained so far you can now start working on large-scale paintings, with broad applications of color. To understand what I mean, look closely at Cézanne's magnificent watercolor reproduced on the following page.

Cézanne showed the way for those painters who later created abstract painting, teaching them how with thought, calculation, continual research and development, it is possible to arrive at the essence of a figure, to reach the model's soul and find a fresh point of view from which to create a new way of painting.

This work by Cézanne is perhaps the clearest example of how to attain method and coherence in the uncertain world of painting, and it may serve as an example to beginners who wish to follow this hard but rewarding discipline.

Talking of beginners, I would like to add that it is a very serious mistake to start painting in a modern style without having acquired a complete mastery of traditional figure drawing. Also, and above all, before following any particular style or school of painting it is essential to have reached maturity as a painter, to have worked with other painters and to have compared one's own work with theirs. You should never be satisfied with what you achieve; only thus will you continue to improve.

Cézanne was not influenced by any other artist. The painters of the preceding generation intrigued him and aroused his enthusiasm, but they did not affect his art. On the other hand, the painters of the following generation took him as a model. Let us turn to the reproduction of his watercolor, which forms part of a series of studies for the famous painting called *The Card-Players*. Nobody could ever have imagined that only a short time later this style of painting would give rise to Cubism and then to abstract painting, which detaches itself from the world of "things as you see them" to enter into the world of "things as you think them." Cézanne's rejection of the aesthetic conventions of his time, which were fundamental to the training of his contemporaries and were dictated by fashion and the contemporary art-market, caused him many problems.

Paul Cézanne: Study of a Card-Player, *ca. 1892, 19⅛×12¾ in. (48.5×32.6 cm), Private collection.*

The painting style of the "innovative" artists was pilloried by the official market, Impressionists, Cubists and abstract artists alike. Because of this attitude these painters were forced to live for many years on the fringe of the official art world, until at last (often after they were dead) their work in turn became official art.

Cézanne used the same working method to paint various subjects, whether still lifes, figures, or landscapes. Each mass of color has a warm area and a cold area, thus color is not seen as a value but as the sum of the cold and warm values it contains. Gray, for instance, can be warm if yellow or red is added, cold if blue or green is added.

In this watercolor (which is simply a color sketch) we can see how the entire figure was washed over all at once so as to give a complete view of all its tones before continuing with any variations. It is also an example of the painter's ability in knowing when a work is "finished." Cézanne left us many "unfinished" watercolors. Looking at them, I am reminded of Michelangelo's love for the *non finito* and of the additional qualities of his unfinished works compared to any other finished work. Far from being *non finito,* they are infinite.

A large-scale portrait in Conté crayon and watercolor

If you want to try a rather special technique you can draw a portrait in Conté crayon. Conté crayons are available in black, bistre, and sanguine.

Drawings done with sanguine have a particular delicacy, which comes from the characteristic burnt ochre color. These crayons may be a little out of fashion, but you can still easily buy them. Working with a sanguine pencil and watercolors, you will find the results are well worthwhile.

Take a very rough paper and draw your figure carefully, slightly shadowing the darker areas if you wish. Use a normal charcoal fixative but do not overdo it, otherwise the colors will run. If you have used too much color, lighten it with ox-gall liquid.

Now, applying the rules of composition we have discussed, try positioning your model, aiming to create a particular mood through the posture of the trunk, the shoulders, arms and hands, the inclination of the head, the direction of the glance, the movement of the hair.

Look carefully at my painting and examine every detail. Note, for example, the important role played by the subject's arms and

97

hands in suggesting an attitude of melancholic expectation. Remember that the surroundings are also important, and therefore carefully select the objects that will be placed near the figure as part of the composition.

In creating atmosphere the determining factor is choice of colors. In my painting most of the colors are on the cold side, which makes the sanguine stand out more. The background I have left incomplete; I merely filled it in round the contours of the figure and vase using Prussian Blue and very little Burnt Umber, and increasing the latter a little in the darker areas. For the half-tones on the blouse I used very dilute Ultramarine Blue and Burnt Umber. In the darker areas I superimposed the same color after the first wash had dried.

The color of the vase was obtained by adding a little Burnt Umber to the Ultramarine Blue used for the blouse.

The hair is a mixture of Raw Sienna and a little Burnt Sienna. For the shadows on the hair I superimposed the same blue I used for the background (Prussian Blue mixed with Burnt Umber). A wash of a little well-diluted Vermilion has been applied to the part of the hair in the foreground.

The flowers were painted with Cadmium Yellow and a little orange in the warmest areas, and the shadows on the petals are Ultramarine Blue and Raw Umber.

I used Raw Sienna and Vermilion for the skin tone. The shadows in the eye area and under the nose were painted with Ultramarine Blue and Burnt Umber. For the cheeks and the tip of the nose I used Vermilion to achieve a warmer tone, while round the mouth I applied a very light wash of Raw Sienna. The light area of the mouth is Vermilion with a little Burnt Sienna; the darker area is Vermilion plus Raw Umber.

The base color I used for the hands is Raw Sienna and Vermilion with a wash of Raw Umber superimposed.

The outlines of the table are traced with Vandyke Brown and Raw Umber.

Another study of the same subject
Now look at the detail of this head with the face resting on the hand, taken from another angle. Notice the same attitude of melancholic expectation: the hand and the way the head is inclined are all that is needed to suggest the same mood as that of the preceding painting. In this example, I can show you how to obtain the same mood with even fewer elements than before and without relying on the

expression of the face, the posture of the mouth, and so on.

You will also have noticed how I altered the colors, making the overall tone a fraction grayer.

The background, which is hinted at with only a few strokes, is a grayish blue made by adding a touch of Ultramarine Blue to Bistre. In the darker areas I superimposed a second wash of the same color immediately after the first had dried.

The hair was painted with a mixture of Burnt Sienna and a drop of heavily diluted Bistre. After the first wash of color had dried, I superimposed a little Burnt Sienna on the warmest parts of the hair. For the shadows on the hair I used a mixture of Burnt Sienna and Bistre, blending the paint into the background.

I applied a wash of pure and well-diluted Ultramarine Blue on to the darkest shadows to increase the depth of tone without the colors blending.

The skin tone on both the hand and the uncovered part of the face was obtained with a mixture of Raw Sienna and Vermilion, applied with a lot of water for maximum transparency.

I applied a wash of Burnt Sienna to the tips of the fingers. Occasional washes of Bistre are superimposed on the back of the hand and on the face to darken the shadow areas.

To complete the painting, I applied a wash of Ultramarine Blue to the darkest parts of the composition.

Copying the same subject from different angles is a very useful exercise that will help you to choose the most harmonious poses.

A SELF-PORTRAIT BY ALDO RAIMONDI

Aldo Raimondi is eighty-two years old, though he doesn't look it. He walks with a quick pace and has a firm handshake, and his eyes light up when one speaks of watercolors. During our meeting he told me of his school of watercolor painting and how, since his retirement, nothing further has been achieved in Italy in this area of figurative art. Aldo Raimondi was a lecturer in watercolor painting at the Brera Academy, the only position of its kind in Italy, from 1939 to 1964.

Most of Raimondi's works are painted on a large scale, and his style is fresh and immediate. He strives continually to perfect his technique and is a true master of watercolor painting.

Talking to Raimondi I learned how, from his youth, he had been fascinated by the works of such artists as Turner, Fattori, and Cremona, and how the discovery of watercolor painting was a revelation to him.

During his long life as a painter Raimondi has painted many portraits of important people from the worlds of politics, religion, and culture; he has also painted self-portraits of great artistic worth, such as the one reproduced here.

Observe closely the transparency and the range of tones that the painter has used, and try to understand how he has come by these effects.

Now paint a self-portrait following the technique used by Aldo Raimondi.

First, position a mirror on the wall so that you have your reflection from the waist up. Place your easel at the minimum distance of about 3 to 5 ft. (1 to 1.50 m) from the mirror, which should be on your left or, if you are left-handed, on your right.

Try not to move your body and mark the position of your feet so that you will always stand in the same place.

Work with big brushes, and use watercolors in tubes and a large sheet of paper. Develop a passion for watercolor painting and work with the same enthusiasm as this artist, who still paints with the same fire and dedication as he has done all his life.

Aldo Raimondi (1903): Self-Portrait, 1982, 19¾×27½ in. (50×70 cm), Artist's collection.

Hands

Besides the features of the face, the role of the hands plays a very important part in every portrait. The great painters of the past made dozens and dozens of studies of hands from life before deciding upon the final position for their models.

Hands, like all other parts of the body, follow a very precise geometry: each positioning of the hands creates different relationships and proportions.

A painter must be able to copy hands very easily, and to achieve that ability he has to make a great many studies of hands.

Look at Leonardo's fascinating studies of hands reproduced here.

Put some tracing paper over Leonardo's drawings and try to work out how he has constructed these hands. Try to find the hidden geometry and the meeting points of imaginary lines exactly as I did for the *Study of Heads* by Watteau.

Painting hands in watercolor

The hands, as I have already said, constitute a composition in themselves. The important thing is that they should be seen as a complete composition with a balanced visual weight and a well-calculated construction; above all

Leonardo da Vinci (1452-1519): Studies of Hands, *Royal Library, Windsor Castle*

they should be copied or painted from life.

Now look carefully at my drawing of hands (fig. 1). For such drawings it is advisable to use a soft pencil (3B) or, if you prefer, Conté crayon.

Now let us move on to the painting (fig. 2).

The first wash is of pure Raw Sienna, heavily diluted. The warm area of the right hand is obtained by adding a little Raw Sienna, a small amount of Burnt Umber, and very little Carmine. The shadow between the thumb, index finger and the palm of the hand is painted with a mixture of a little Burnt Umber and a drop of Ultramarine Blue.

I got the shadow of the wrist by mixing some Burnt Umber and Ultramarine Blue in equal quantities.

Under the thumb is an area of very light shadow, still painted with Ultramarine Blue, but with a higher percentage of Burnt Umber.

The index finger, the middle finger, and those parts of the ring finger and little finger that you can only see contain a little Raw Umber as well as Ultramarine Blue and Burnt Umber.

I also used Raw Sienna as a base for the left hand, the warmest area being created with Burnt Umber and a little Ultramarine Blue.

For the back of the hand I used the same mix of colors, but increased the percentage of blue. I added more light washes, with further additions of blue the closer I got to the darker areas.

The shadow of the cloth was painted with Bistre to which a little Ultramarine Blue was added.

Eyes

Now let's examine another very important feature in the composition of a portrait: the eyes. As a first step I suggest you obtain some reproductions of portraits by the great artists. Examine the ways the eyes have been painted or drawn and then, using the same techniques, practice copying eyes from life.

Remember that the eyes move parallel to each other and that this parallelism must be maintained and controlled in your drawing. Indeed, even a tiny error in construction can make your subject appear to squint.

The following exercise is divided into four parts. The first concerns the drawing of the eyes and the shadowing.

The second looks at the preparation of the base colors: Raw Sienna and Vermilion for the flesh, a diluted Bistre for the pupils, a diluted Ultramarine Blue for the iris with a superimposition of well-diluted Emerald

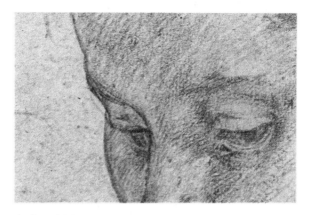

Andrea del Sarto (1486-1531): Portrait of a Girl *(detail)*

Leonardo: Studies of Two Warriors' Heads *(detail)*

Raphael (1483-1520): Head of a Youth *(detail)*

Green towards the center of the eye and, for the shadow in the white of the eye, a greatly diluted Vandyke Brown.

The third part deals with accentuating the dark areas. Add Burnt Umber to Raw Sienna to darken the eyelids and the tear ducts of the eye, and the darkest part of the pupil. Superimpose a wash of Bistre at the outside of the iris, and add further washes of Ultramarine Blue.

The fourth part consists of emphasizing the darkest areas by superimposing the more or less diluted base colors and giving light, shadows, and reflections to the eye as if it were a crystal object. You must pay special attention to making the eyes look "live."

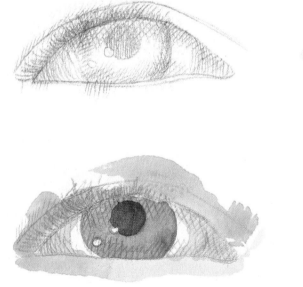

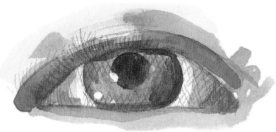

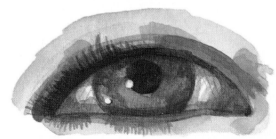

Ears

Inexperienced painters usually tend to neglect the ears. But these curious features should be studied closely and, again, the portraits of great painters should be carefully examined. Look at the details of faces, "read" them, and then go on to copy them from a model.

Try drawing ears from different angles, and when you begin painting them, pay attention to the various planes you can create with shadows.

Andrea del Sarto: Portrait of a Girl *(detail)*

Andrea del Sarto: Profile of a Young Man *(detail)*

Leonardo: Studies of Two Warriors' Heads

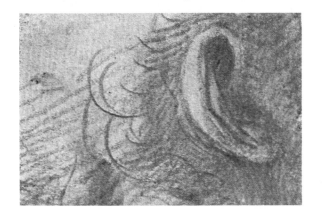

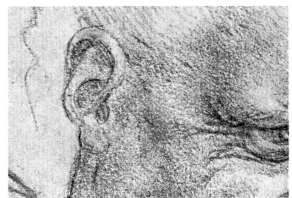

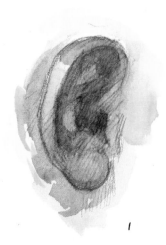

Nose

When you come to paint the nose the advice is the same as for the eyes and ears: copy from the masters first.

Start by copying noses with special characteristics — big, pimpled, flat, aquiline — and study the length, the shape of the nostrils, etc. Then, when you have mastered these, study more normal noses and copy them from every angle — from the front, above, below, in profile, and so on.

This is how you should proceed with the exercise (fig. 1): draw the details, then apply the first wash of Raw Sienna and Vermilion over the whole area.

Now add Burnt Umber to the warmer areas and superimpose Ultramarine Blue in the darker areas.

The concave areas of the ear must not be too dark, or they will look like holes instead of depressions.

Leonardo: Studies of Two Warriors' Heads *(detail)*

Leonardo: Studies of Two Warriors' Heads *(detail)*

Lorenzo di Credi (1459-1527): Head of a Young Man *(detail)*

Michelangelo (1475-1564): Study of a Head *(detail)*

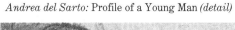

Andrea del Sarto: Profile of a Young Man *(detail)*

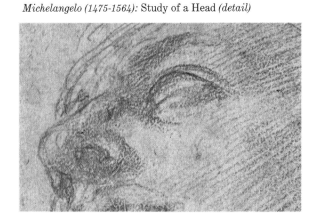

109

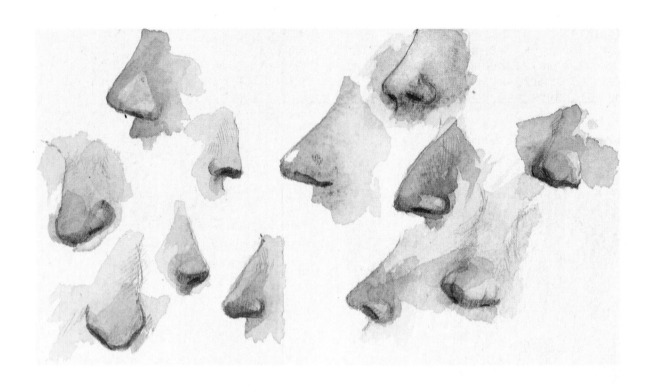

Draw all the noses you come across, as I have done in this exercise. Begin with a very simple combination of colors: Raw Sienna and Vermilion for the flesh, washes of Ultramarine Blue for the shadows. Make as many of these studies as you can, filling sketchbooks with notes and examples, working first on a small scale and then on a larger scale. Study the play of light on the nose, and experiment with both cold and warm tones.

Mouth

After the eyes, the mouth is the most expressive part of the face. Copy as many as possible from life, also looking at paintings of the old masters.

Leonardo: Studies of Two Warriors' Heads *(detail)*

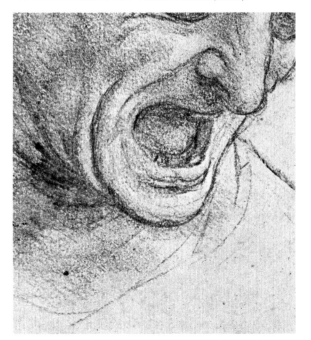

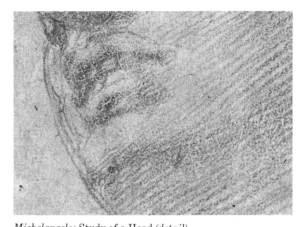

Michelangelo: Study of a Head *(detail)*

Lorenzo di Credi: Head of a Young Man *(detail)*

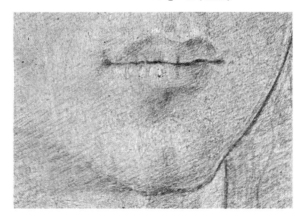

Examine the mouths that I have painted as examples. Be very careful to balance the shadow areas and always emphasize the difference in color between one lip and the other. Remember that in normal light the upper lip always has a darker shadow than the lower.

To give the impression of wet lips, leave a small area unpainted on the lower lip so that the white of the paper will look like a reflection.

When the mouth is open and the teeth can be seen, never leave them completely white but wash them with a very transparent Bistre, otherwise they will stand out too much and will look like a strip of white plaster placed on the lips.

The colors used for this study are Vermilion mixed with a small drop of Raw Sienna. For the shadows you have to add a little Ultramarine Blue to the mixture or apply a wash of Ultramarine Blue when the base color is dry.

Elsewhere the shadows can be created by superimposing Raw Umber on to the underlying color when it is dry.

With thin lips, the shadows are more emphasized and there is hardly any difference in shape between the upper and the lower lips.

Hair

To paint hair in watercolor it is necessary first to draw a bald head and then cover it with hair, noting the thickness and whether it is straight, wavy, or curly. Do the darker shadows first in pencil and then cover them with washes of the darkest shade of color.

Raphael: Studies of Warriors *(detail)*

113

You can also superimpose colors before the base color is dry, working delicately with the tip of the brush. When the paint is dry add the finishing touches, using a very diluted pure blue for the areas which need to be darkened but which, at the same time, should remain transparent.

The light areas are treated in the same way but with warmer colors.

Never underestimate the importance of the hair in a portrait. Work carefully, for if you paint the hair poorly you will spoil the whole portrait.

Fair hair should be painted Cadmium Yellow as a base, the half-tones are obtained by using Burnt Umber, while for the darker shadows you should add a touch of Raw Umber.

For brown hair, paint the lighter areas with Burnt Sienna and the darker areas with washes of Turquoise Blue.

If the hair is black, work with Bistre and washes of Carmine in the lighter areas, and Bistre and washes of Ultramarine Blue in the darker areas.

Grey hair is created by using the white of the paper for the lighter areas and washing the darker areas with heavily diluted Bistre. Remember that grey hair easily reflects the surrounding colors.

114

THE NUDE

Learning to draw the nude has been perhaps the greatest aspiration of painters of all times.

To understand how important the old masters considered the nude, we need only read what Leonardo da Vinci wrote about it in his *Treatise on Painting,* in the chapter dealing with the importance to artists of the study of anatomy:

"It is necessary for the painter, if he is to be a good portrayer of the attitudes and gestures of the nude figure, to know the anatomy of the nerves, bones, and muscles, so that he will know, for the different movements and tensions, what nerves or muscles are responsible for them, and emphasize those alone and not the others, as do many artists who, wanting to seem great draftsmen, make their nudes look stiff and graceless, more like bags of walnuts than human flesh, bunches of radishes rather than muscular nudes."

Leonardo carries on warning the "anatomical painter" to beware of overdoing the bones, tendons, and muscles, for his figure will be stiff if he pays too much attention to every minute detail of the body's structure. To overcome this danger, he advises, in drawing old and thin people one should take care to have the muscles "cover and dress" the bones completely and not leave uncovered even the spaces between the muscles. One must also know which muscles are always visible and which, on the other hand, disappear with even the slightest relaxation. Remember, furthermore (Leonardo continues), that often in fat people several muscles look like one, while in thin people one muscle looks like many.

Later, speaking of beauty and grace, of balance and proportion, Leonardo states that whoever does not have the gift of giving his figures a beautiful expression can learn to do so by study.

The painter, he advises, should copy the best parts of beautiful faces, commonly accepted as such and not considered beautiful by himself alone, for he may deceive himself by copying faces that are similar to his own. It often happens, says Leonardo, that an unattractive person chooses unattractive faces, as do many painters whose models, in fact, closely resemble them.

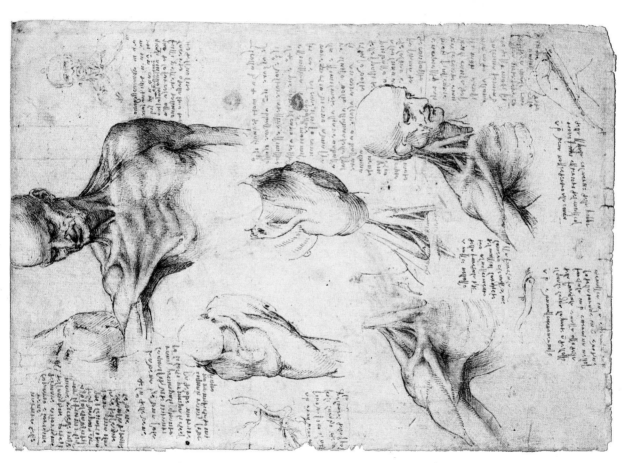

A STUDY IN WATERCOLOR BY CARL LARSSON

Carl Larsson was a Swedish painter and engraver, and one of the most important watercolorists living at the end of the nineteenth century and the beginning of the twentieth.

His method of work was the same as that of the great painters of every era: first the nude is drawn in pencil or charcoal, then it is etched or engraved with a drypoint, and finally it is colored.

This is what Larsson wrote in the magazine *Kunst* (1911): "...it would be enough reward if only men, through my art, understood how beautiful a flower on the side of a path is; how charming are the plaits around a young girl's small round neck, and the touch of the sun on a little nose; how splendid the nude figure of a woman is, with a man and a horse on the horizon... but one must produce these images in the best possible way, with joy and enthusiasm, with hard work and pain, and the final result must be a victory, not giving the impression of confusion or fatigue, but illuminating the onlooker in a liberating way... Following this way of life, painters executed study after study,

without being pleased or satisfied with their work, striving to reach that perfection which always seemed further away with each work that they were painting."

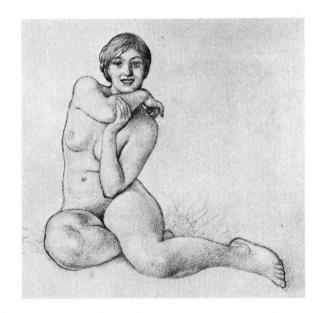

Carl Larsson (1853-1919): Girl Crouching, *1911, drawing, Konstmuseum, Göteborg*

118

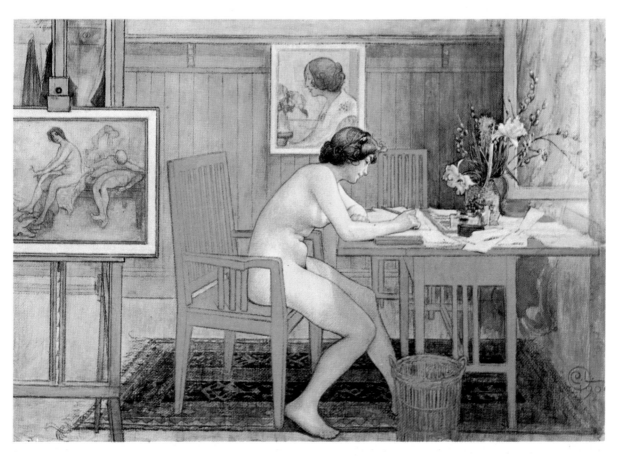

Carl Larsson: Model Writing a Picture Postcard, *1906, Thielska Gallery, Stockholm.*

Practising painting the nude

For the nude, as for the figure, it is best to start on a small scale.

Always work from life and try to make the model adopt natural poses.

If in the beginning you find this difficult, suggest that the model poses like the nudes of the old masters.

In time you will be able to give the necessary directions.

You will discover that the great artists painted even the smallest detail, and if a single detail in their work didn't satisfy them, they went closer to the model and repeated it many times, enlarging it, on the edge of the paper.

I would advise beginners to start practising with the female nude, preferably using a model who is not too thin.

You will find that a thin model is very difficult to paint, for it requires a great knowledge of anatomy.

The male model is more difficult than the female for the same reason.

Make your first studies with the model standing in profile. Try to work quickly and stop every ten to fifteen minutes to allow the model to rest. Before she takes her rest mark the exact position of her feet with chalk or charcoal so that when you resume work after the break she will stand in exactly the same position as before.

When you have gained enough experience move on to a frontal pose, with the model first standing then seated. Draw quickly but with precision, and then begin painting at once, using all the techniques that I have taught you. Superimpose each wash while the previous one is still damp, working the paint delicately with the brush. Let the paint dry before you add the final wash.

The colors used for the skin tone are Raw Sienna and a drop of Vermilion for the basic tone; for the pinker areas add a little Carmine to the ground color, and for the shadows Ultramarine Blue with a drop of Carmine.

The half-tones can be washed with a little Turquoise Blue.

Mixing Vandyke Brown and Ultramarine Blue will give you the color for the hair.

The examples are reproduced to the same size as the originals. I suggest you paint several nude studies.

Try to arrange the lighting so that the shadows are emphasized. Remember to build up the shadows meticulously; take care not to darken them too much, otherwise they will look like holes.

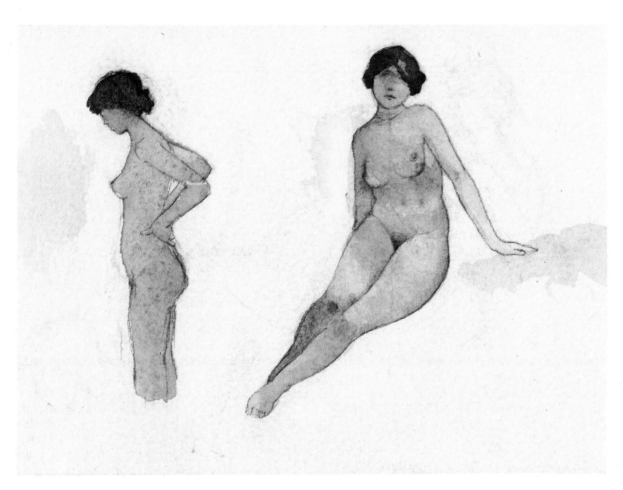

FROM ONE OF CEZANNE'S SKETCHBOOKS

Looking carefully at the small study called *Three Women Bathers* (dealing with a theme which recurs many times in Cézanne's painting) one notices straight away that the artist doesn't use color to simply represent colored objects and scenes, but rather as a means to create sensations. In fact these figures, which we at once "read" as flesh, were painted with every color except that of flesh.

Cézanne is regarded as an Impressionist painter, but the only thing he shares with the Impressionists is in fact the period in which he lived.

His color does not express visual reality but an atmosphere of color. The color is split into minute fragments, resulting in a transparent mosaic effect. Each brush stroke is carefully placed to build up a shape. Even space is not submitted to a perspective construction but rather to a perspective vision, the small colored segments combining to make up a structure of colored masses seen in perspective.

Space is thus no longer defined by a rigid rule, but is something mutable that obeys the laws of time and is constantly transformed.

Cézanne wrote: "Treat Nature according to the cylinder, the cone, and the sphere, all seen in perspective." This sentence anticipates the basic theory of the Cubist movement.

Strictly allied to Cézanne's vision of space is his vision of color. He goes on to say "...Nature, for man, is rather more in depth than on the surface, whence the necessity to introduce into our vibrations of light, represented by reds and yellows, a quantity of bluish tones to suggest the atmosphere..."

The watercolor reproduced here is not, therefore, reality as Cézanne saw it, but rather as he "felt" it and how he would express it in his final painting.

Cézanne's experience with watercolors had a fundamental effect on his art, influencing even his oil paintings. Watercolors were to Cézanne what the frescoes were to the great Renaissance painters.

Cézanne gave up everything to dedicate himself to his art, and his art became his life. For him there was no such thing as a social problem – only the problem of painting existed. His subjects were not derived from the world about him, but from his inner life.

Paul Cézanne: Three Women Bathers, *1874/76, The National Museum of Wales, Cardiff.*

Keeping a sketchbook of nude studies

You can find numerous subjects for studies to fill your sketchpad. On the beach, or on the banks of rivers and lakes, you can observe people lying, standing, or sitting in all kinds of positions. Make rapid sketches of these positions and then ask a model to pose in the same way.

First draw the subject very lightly, then use pure, transparent, sunny colors to just cover the pencilled outline that should show through the paint.

For the first exercise I copied a fat man sunbathing in a deckchair on the beach.

While I was drawing; the "model" changed position twice. I took advantage of this to do another study.

You, too, should not be put out if your subject changes position while you are drawing; rather, you should see it as an opportunity to do another study and as a challenge to work even more quickly.

The second and third studies were done on a riverbank. The drawings were made with just a few light lines. I used a limited range of colors of a very luminous kind. By now you should have sufficient understanding of color to work out for yourself what colors I have used.

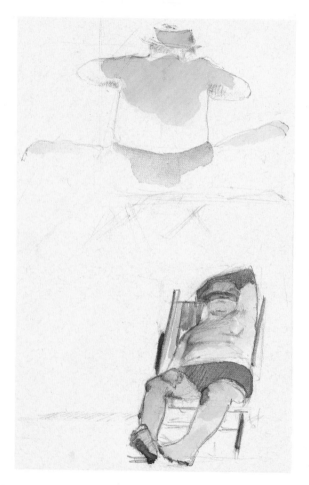

"GIRL SLEEPING ON THE BANKS OF THE MARNE" BY ANDRE PLANSON

Planson did not only paint the ballet and dancers in the wings of the Opéra or at the music hall. He was also, and primarily, the painter of the Marne. Far more important to him than the attractions of Paris were the strong bonds that tied him to his birthplace and to those things he was most familiar with. Planson loved to work from life, and he always took with him on his walks the equipment for watercolor painting and a sketchbook. He painted meadows and cultivated fields, the banks of the Marne, the fishermen and oarsmen, the boats and bridges, and the people dancing by the light of colored lamps.

Planson's love of the river is related to his love of the female form. The female nude, sleeping languidly on the banks of the Marne, her drowsy puppy lying by her arm, with a violet-red cap over her brown hair and a blue cloth around her waist, is like a nymph of the woods. In the background, outlined in green paint, we can discern a small boat with two people rowing.

The colors are lively, almost primary colors; but not one relates to the water of the river on which the boatmen row — it is the atmosphere of the painting, rather, which makes us "feel" that the water is there. Now look at this work with your eyes half closed. You will see how the colors come alive and how, by an optical effect, the white area of the river acquires a light blue tinge while the grass is filled with reflections of light.

This painting also shows how useful it is to have your watercolors always at hand. So take your paints, go out, and observe and copy everything that will help you learn and add to your experience, all the poses you will ask your models to adopt when you are back in your studio. Remember that often life-studies can work well on a small scale, but when they are reproduced on a larger scale they are less satisfactory.

Always bear in mind that the poses you choose for your sketches must also work on a larger scale. The way to find out in advance what your design will look like when enlarged is very simple: look carefully at your chosen subject and, if you see it enclosed in an ideal geometric figure (rectangle, triangle, etc.), you can be sure that it will reproduce well in any size.

André Planson (1898): Sleeping Girl on the Banks of the Marne, *1967, 9×12½ in. (23×32 cm),* Private collection, Lausanne.

ANIMALS

In learning to draw animals it is essential that your subject be as motionless as possible. You can start by copying equestrian monuments or stuffed animals in a natural history museum, or the geese, ducks, pheasants, chickens, and rabbits you have bought for your dinner. Copying a dead animal, though it may seem somewhat macabre, will help you to get to know it in detail. Equally useful is the study of seventeenth-century Flemish still life, in which paintings of game abound.

When you have enough experience, turn to your own or your neighbors' pets while they are asleep. If you live in the country you will be able to make studies of chickens and rabbits and, even better, horses and cows. When you have had sufficient practice you can set off with your sketchpad to paint animals as they move about.

Practise first by making very small watercolor sketches of animals in motion. The easiest ones to start with are aquatic animals, first because there is only half the animal to copy (the other half being below the water surface), and secondly because aquatic animals move harmoniously.

128

Study the watercolor reproduced here. Keep your eyes half closed as you look and paint. A few strokes are sufficient for this tiny study. Use just a few colors and, since the sketch is so small, don't spoil it with too many superimposed washes.

The dominant color is Ultramarine Blue. The water and the swan are both painted in the same color, varying only in density.

After a little practice you can try painting a different water bird: a mallard makes a beautiful subject. In my exercise I have subdivided the body of the mallard into three parts to show how you can work in stages.

In the first stage, wash the drawing with the background color, starting from the water.

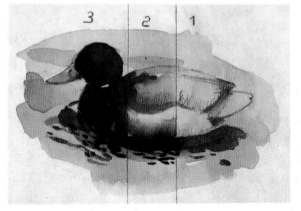

Mix a little Emerald Green with a drop of Ultramarine Blue and quickly apply the paint to the area of the water. Add a little more Ultramarine Blue to the color you have already mixed, diluting it more, and paint the body of the bird. Add to the same color a small amount of Raw Umber, making the paint slightly thicker, and paint the dark reflection; then use the same mix to go over the darkest parts, such as the tips of the wings and the shadows on the wings. If you work quickly, before the paint underneath has dried, you can obtain the special effect you see in the picture reproduced here.

In the second stage accentuate the colors, darkening the mallard and going over it again with the same colors as in the first phase, but emphasizing the warm areas by adding a drop of Burnt Sienna to the base color, and applying washes to the bird's back. Paint the head by mixing Emerald Green with Burnt Umber and, with a very diluted wash, cover the green area of the head completely. Paint the beak with heavily diluted Cadmium Yellow.

In the last stage all the colors are strengthened, using thicker washes. If you work quickly enough the colors will blend, creating an attractive effect.

Aldo Raimondi: Calf, *1976, 19¾×27½ in. (50×70 cm), Private collection.*

ALDO RAIMONDI'S ANIMAL PAINTINGS

Aldo Raimondi is an artist who has kept the freshness of spirit of a twenty-year-old. An unpretentious man who likes unpretentious subjects, he seems to see everything as if for the first time and finds inspiration in simple things. Raimondi never tires of exploring the possibilities of his art, and he is still making new discoveries. He has painted watercolor portraits of many great people, from Ettore Petrolini to Peppino de Filippo, from Pope Pius XII to Paul VI and John XXIII.

"Although I have painted the portraits of many famous people," he says, "I love even more to paint landscapes, still lifes, and animals — their shapes, their movements and their disconcerting expressions. I like to paint them quickly and with a sure hand: in fact, a watercolor is more pleasing when the drops of color remain intact and the colors are less elaborate. I have never followed any particular school, and sometimes I am considered old-fashioned because I look for my subjects in a cow-shed, a circus, a meadow, or a garden... I find the attraction of a landscape, a flower or a rural scene irresistible."

He continues with a concise judgment on watercolor painting: "With this means the didactic intention is pre-eminent; it could not be otherwise. In fact, if at a decisive point in my life I left active teaching, the artist in me never suppressed the teacher.

"To succeed in watercolors (within the limits of an essentially didactic purpose), an absolute command of drawing is paramount. Working with watercolors means drawing continuously with a brush, until a high level of skill is achieved... The immediacy of the tones can give value even to one single watery mark, which can become as significant as the most subtle of nuances. The white of the paper and a genuine superimposition of the transparent colors with no second thoughts or artifice of any kind contribute to the beauty of a pure watercolor. The English, great connoisseurs and admirers of this form of painting, used to examine watercolors against the light to make sure there were no superimpositions of white lead or tempera.

"To become a proficient watercolor painter one needs tenacity, a long and hard apprenticeship, and much humility, as the old philosophers have taught us."

Painting cats

Cats are the animals I most like to paint. They are also the most difficult. A cat's movements are always smooth; the curves and forms of its body, whether at rest, running, or fighting, are quite magical. Set yourself the challenge of painting a cat.

Start by copying cats while they are asleep, for it is much easier to draw their bodies when they are relaxed. (No other sleeping animal looks quite as relaxed as a cat.) If the drawing has not been done well, the cat's body will appear stiff and lacking in softness.

When you feel sure you have learned enough about the cat while it is asleep, try to sketch it in motion.

Draw quickly, without hesitation, and observe carefully the way it moves. Follow the cat while you draw, and you will find that it adopts the same position three or four times. This should be enough for you to finish your sketches.

You can also try working directly with a brush, without doing a pencil drawing first. Use the brush as if it were a pen with a nib, making use of the flexibility of the hairs and varying the pressure to broaden or taper the areas of paint.

The first cat (top left) was painted with Bistre with a small addition of Ultramarine Blue. Cadmium Yellow was used for the eyes. The second cat, caught jumping over a low wall, was painted directly with the brush, using Bistre with a little Turquoise Blue added. The third cat was also painted directly with a brush.

This restful pose, with the front paws folded under the chest, presents an easier subject. I drew the outline with Bistre, using the tip of the brush, then worked the body using more of the flat of the brush. For the eye I used Cadmium Yellow.

The cat in the top right-hand corner was also painted directly with the brush. The Bistre was applied much more thickly than in the previous example (but it must never be used as thickly as tempera). If you find the color is not dark enough, go over it a second time before the first wash dries out.

The striped cat eyeing a bird was first drawn in pencil and then painted. For the darker stripes I used a mixture of Bistre and just a little Raw Sienna to give a tinge of green. I superimposed a wash of Raw Sienna on the lighter areas of the body and face.

The cat running was sketched with a soft pencil (6B) and a smudge of Burnt Umber washed over it.

Painting horses

Now try drawing a more difficult animal. A horse is a good example. Get hold of a reproduction of the bone structure of a horse or draw its skeleton in a natural history museum, studying it carefully.

Then go on to copy drawings of horses by the great masters.

When you think you understand the structure of the horse, you can try to draw from life. Sketch the horse in motion, drawing first you immediate impression, and then finish the drawing using what you have learned about the horse. This system can speed up your learning capacity. Naturally you must keep on drawing without being discouraged by initial setbacks.

When you are in the country, you may find some draught-horses pulling carts. You will notice that their movements are restricted. When the horses are feeding, their movements are quite slow, and you can make studies of them more easily. When you are sufficiently skilled you can go on to draw those nervous and elegant animals, race horses.

All these exercises should be carried out at first on a small scale, increasing gradually to larger and larger scales.

LANDSCAPES

After working for a long time in a studio, the watercolorist feels an almost physical need to paint a landscape. For landscape painting you need to know and apply the rules of perspective. For the first few attempts at outdoor painting, choose a day when the sky is overcast and there are fewer contrasts and fewer dissonant shadows. Work on a small scale and choose evocative views. Do your first paintings in spring rather than in summer — the large patches of green make a landscape easier to study. Autumn and winter landscapes, with masses of red and yellow leaves and bare trees, present a more difficult task, which is better tackled when you have really mastered the technique.

It is better to start with details and only gradually pass on to entire scenes. Before you go out and look for your landscape, make yourself a cardboard viewfinder of proportionally smaller dimensions than your sheet of paper. Once you have chosen your subject, look at it with the viewfinder held a little away from your eyes, framing the view.

To reduce or enlarge a format

To make a proportional reduction of a rectangle, trace a diagonal line joining two opposite corners. Mark along the base line of the rectangle the length of the new format (the length you want your viewfinder to be). Now trace a vertical line, at right-angles to the base line, from this mark up to the diagonal line. Then, from where these two lines join, trace a horizontal line, parallel to the base line, to meet the left-hand vertical line. The rectangle you have drawn is propor-

tionally smaller than the original rectangle.

If, on the other hand, you want a format proportionally bigger than the original, follow the same procedure as for a reduction but go beyond the dimensions of the original rectangle, extending the diagonal line and the base line as far as necessary to accomodate the new format. To find the height of the new rectangle, draw a vertical line, as before, to the point where it crosses the diagonal.

The landscape painter needs a second type of viewfinder, made with a wooden frame and thick string nailed across it. Use the proportional method explained above for its con-

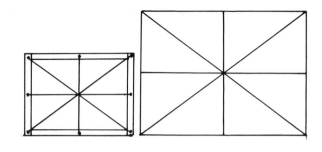

struction. Assemble the frame following the illustrations on this page and nail the string so that it dissects the rectangle. Copy these intersecting lines on to your sheet of paper. Nail the frame on to a stick and stand it upright so that the frame is at eye level.

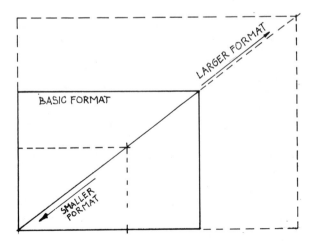

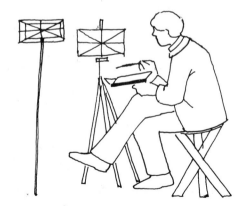

EXTRACTS FROM THE LETTERS OF VAN GOGH

In one of his letters to his brother Théo, Van Gogh refers to a "perspective frame" he made from an idea first conceived by Albrecht Dürer. But while Dürer only used the frame in his studio, Van Gogh used it for his landscape paintings.

Van Gogh writes: "Though it is true that during the winter I spent less on paints than the other artists, I spent more on constructing an instrument for the study of proportion and perspective which I found described in a book by Albrecht Dürer and which the old Dutch masters also used. This implement allows you to compare the nearer and the more distant objects in those cases where it is not possible to draw according to the rules of perspective. When one relies on the eye alone, the result is invariably wrong. I wasn't successful at once in making it, but finally I succeeded after many attempts with the help of the carpenter and the blacksmith. And after further effort I can see the possibility of achieving even better results."

Reading Van Gogh's letter to his brother we begin to understand with how much love, passion, constancy, and sacrifice the painter lived and faced his life as an artist day by day. Let me now quote another letter in which Van Gogh speaks of the watercolor reproduced on the following page. It is an extraordinary letter. I have read it many times and each time it has moved me deeply. The painting itself speaks better than my words. It is one of the artist's first works. His progress as an artist, the alterations he made to the colors

Vincent Van Gogh: The Beach at Scheveningen, *1882, Vincent Van Gogh Foundation, Amsterdam*

on his palette and the quality of his oil paintings should not blind us to the fact that Van Gogh was, above all, a great watercolorist.

"Dear Théo,
I have just received your letter with 50 francs enclosed, for which I thank you very much. I enclose some small, new watercolor paintings. As you will remember, one day when you were here you remarked that I should try to send you a small painting of the 'sellable' type. However, you must excuse me because I don't know exactly when a painting is or isn't 'sellable'. Once I thought I knew, but each day I realize how wrong I am.
Well, I hope that this small bench, even if it is not yet a painting which will sell, will show you that I am not against choosing, at times, pleasant and attractive subjects, and thus it will be easier to find buyers for them than for paintings of a sadder mood.
Together with the bench I include another painting as a *pendant,* also of the woods.
This is the second bench; the first is a larger watercolor I am working on, in which the tone of color is more gloomy, but I don't know if I'll succeed in finishing it well. ...I like to do these sketches and ...I would like to perfect them as much as possible. I beg you to remember that just a little more money helps me to make more progress than I would be able to achieve otherwise.
One needs many things and everything is so expensive. But in any case I am doubly grateful to you and I feel more fortunate than the others because of the money I receive from you, and I assure you I do my very best to make progress.
Today I will once more go to the usual Monday market and try to do some sketches while they are unloading the carts.
Good-bye and good luck.
Write to me soon. You know I always like to read your descriptions, like that of Montmartre.
I am handling so much paint that there is even some on this letter. I'm busy on the big watercolor depicting the bench. I would so like it if I succeeded, but the great difficulty is to keep to the correct form and maintain the gloomy colors at the same time; it is very difficult to keep the form evident.
Once more, good-bye...
Heartfelt thanks for having sent me the money when you yourself are short. I have double need of it because autumn is almost over and it is the most beautiful season to paint."

Vincent Van Gogh: The Bench *(from a letter to his brother Théo),* Vincent Van Gogh National Museum, Amsterdam.

Small-scale landscapes

You should begin practicing landscape painting on a small scale.

The watercolor reproduced here was painted on a gray day, which makes the colors easier to see and the light constant for many hours.

The experience that you have gained so far should enable you to work rapidly, using a rich and varied range of colors.

To begin with, choose distant subjects like these houses on a hilltop. I painted them in a range of greens to which I added a drop of Cerulean Blue to convey the subdued gray atmosphere that is typical of a cloudy day. Even in the colors of the houses and the roofs there is a hint of Cerulean Blue.

The fields are Emerald Green with a small addition of Burnt Umber and just a drop of Cerulean Blue.

The darker areas in the trees have been painted with Emerald Green and a small drop of Carmine.

The houses are Burnt Sienna with a slight addition of Cerulean Blue. The blue must be used with great care, strongly diluted, because it must only affect the color, not change it.

Finally, for the roof I used a mixture of Burnt Umber and Cerulean Blue.

140

A landscape from close by

This watercolor showing a view on Lake Molveno is more detailed than the previous example.

The base color is Emerald Green with an addition of Raw Sienna for the warmer area and the trees with the lighter foliage, and of Burnt Sienna for the darker trees.

The foliage immediately beneath the warm area is in shade and reflects the water of the lake: to paint this I added to the Emerald Green a little Ultramarine Blue, a little Carmine and also a drop of Turquoise Blue for the reflections produced by the lake water.

For the lake I used Turquoise Blue as the base color adding a little Ultramarine Blue and a touch of Burnt Umber. The lighter areas of the shore are Raw Sienna, with a little Raw Umber added for the darker areas.

For the trees at the sides of the house I used Emerald Green mixed with Ultramarine Blue, and Burnt Umber.

For the house I used a mixture of Raw Sienna with a small drop of Raw Umber.

The roof was painted in heavily diluted Raw Umber.

Finally, for the more distant trees that can just be seen fading away on the hillside, I used a highly diluted darker green.

Detail of a landscape

Every small detail in a landscape that attracts our attention can itself become a landscape.

This boat on the banks of Lake Molveno is an example.

I had to sketch this quickly because it was constantly moving on the water.

For the pier, which is the darkest part of the composition, I used Bistre with a touch of Burnt Umber.

Adding a little Ultramarine Blue I drew the circle of the car tire, which served as a buffer for the boat. I painted the boat with Bistre mixed with heavily diluted Turquoise Blue, and for the darker shadows on the boat I added a little Bistre.

The rear part of the boat is washed with Raw Umber; for the blue stripe which is painted round the boat I mixed some Ultramarine Blue with a little Carmine, and with the same blue, heavily diluted, I painted the misty background.

For the lake water I used a very diluted wash of the color I used for the stripe.

When this was dry I painted the reflection of the boat on the water in the same colors I used for the boat, accentuating the ripples of the waves with a deeper tone.

Painting sailing boats

On the same day I also painted a series of studies of sailing boats, in the same size as they are reproduced here.

Notice how only a few strokes were quite sufficient to make these small studies effective and evocative, while the background, which I left white, suggests the perspective depth of a landscape.

For the first of the two boats I used a very simple range of colors: Turquoise Blue mixed with a little Ultramarine Blue for the water, the reflection of the sail, and the mast. The same color I used for the water, with the addition of a little Bistre applied to the sail. For the side of the boat I used Burnt Umber mixed with a drop of Carmine, and for the top part of the boat, which reflects the sunlight, I used pure Raw Sienna.

The second boat was painted with just one color, Ultramarine Blue, in various dilutions for the different areas: very diluted for the sail, slightly thicker for the mast. For the boat I laid three washes of Ultramarine Blue, letting the paint dry between each wash to obtain the depth of color. For the reflection in the water I used a blue wash a fraction darker than the blue on the sail, adding a tiny drop of Carmine to the paint.

143

A SEASCAPE BY J.M.W. TURNER

Turner's watercolors never lose their fascination, however many times one looks at them. He was without doubt the greatest English watercolorist. A painter of light, Turner used extraordinary colors, often applied pure, and never failed to suggest depth, air, and luminous transparency. His drawings, ultimately, are pure light and color.

The English writer and art critic John Ruskin recognized in Turner the painter who anticipated the discoveries of the Impressionists, especially in the depiction of light and color.

Turner began by copying the works of Alexander Cozens. Then he went to work at the house of a doctor who possessed a large art collection, and he studied and copied those works.

Copying other painters played a decisive role in Turner's development as a watercolorist; in fact, it gave him the chance to understand in depth the problems of composition and structure, and the secrets of technical skill and varying color tones. Turner's style changed over the years as he gradually learned new techniques and explored new possibilities. When he drew outdoors he discovered hidden depths and new dimensions of light, concerning himself almost exclusively with landscapes.

Scotland, England, the river Thames, and later Italy, Como, Venice, Rome, the Alpine passes — these are the subjects of over 19,000 drawings.

How did Turner draw? We have the evidence left by his friend Farington, who wrote in his diary:

"Light is created by painting over the areas that he wishes to illuminate with a wet brush (a general background has already been applied with a deep colour where necessary), and with some blotting paper heightening the resulting wet color. After this he recleans the area with pieces of bread. Any other color could now be applied here. White chalk is now used to heighten the forms which must be illuminated. A rough and full form can be obtained by passing a camel-hair brush over these forms, which reduces the dampness of the area thus touched so that only those areas affected by the blotting paper are heightened."

J. M. W. Turner (1775-1851): View of Venice from the Giudecca at Dawn, *1819, 8¾×11⅝ in. (22.2×28.8 cm), British Museum, London.*

A LANDSCAPE BY CEZANNE

From 1865 the Impressionist painters around Pissarro (Cézanne, Renoir, Manet, Gauguin, Sisley, and Dégas) had eliminated from their palettes colors such as Bistre, Raw and Burnt Sienna and Umber, and had begun to work solely with the three primary colors, which to them were Ultramarine Blue, Cadmium Yellow, Carmine, and their immediate derivatives: green (blue + yellow), a warm yellow (red + yellow) and violet (blue + red).

From 1874 onwards, for many years, the paintings they exhibited were ridiculed and despised. For this reason Cézanne spent the rest of this life painting in the south of France, in the seclusion of his studio at Les Lauves, on a hilltop above Aix-en-Provence. In the last years of his life watercolors became an integral part of his work and were the pinnacle of his achievement.

Cézanne's watercolors give the impression of being confidently composed and rapidly executed. One can see the brush strokes, applied with orderly logic, and the superimposed washes that the sun of the south would quickly dry.

Like all the Impressionists, he painted landscapes in bright light with marked contrasts of light and shade and deep shadows.

Look at Cézanne's watercolor reproduced here: the first thing to notice is that at this stage the painter considered his work "finished." The drawing fills the entire page. The outlines are painted in violet, and note that the foliage of the trees contains more violet than green or yellow. A few dabs of blue are dotted here and there and the wall of the house is painted with a warm yellow. Incredible, fantastic colors.

Now try looking at the picture with half-closed eyes: you will find that all the violet tones take on a brilliant green sheen; you can verify this by looking at the painting from a distance, with your eyes fully open.

Experience these effects by going out at midday in high summer into a sun-filled field. Paint with your eyes half closed, in full sunlight, the colors that you see or you think you see; you will thus relive the great experiences of the Impressionist painters.

Paul Cézanne: Jourdan's Cabin, *1906, 18⅞ × 24⅝ in. (48 × 62.6 cm), Private collection.*

BOATS BY ALDO RAIMONDI

When you next walk on the beach or along the shore of a lake look at the boats, observe where the sky meets the water, watch the clouds in the distance, the mountains that surround the lake: these are the landscapes of Aldo Raimondi and they are views that we can all see and enjoy.

His landscapes communicate neither anguish nor torment, but rather a sense of peace and serenity and the joy that fills the soul of one who sees and loves Nature in all its aspects.

Look at this watercolor by Raimondi; note its translucence, the reflections on the water and the peaceful atmosphere rendered with such simplicity.

When you are outdoors painting a landscape like this, keep the book open at this page and try to imitate Raimondi's technique. Don't copy, but work out how he created certain effects and achieved certain color tones. As I have said many times, studying and understanding how a master watercolorist works will help you greatly in your own painting. It is even useful to imitate his techniques until you have developed your own style. Be guided by the experience of this great teacher: observe the angle and composition he choose, the space occupied by the boats and the water, the reflection of the boats floating on the rippled water. Each brush stroke, as well as applying the paint, also builds up form. For example, see how, by superimposing washes, the brush has created each detail of the boat with sails hoisted. See, too, how the artist succeeded in creating some very vivid effects, which reminds us of the vibrating works of the *Macchiaioli*.

Learn to paint in the foreground in darker tones than those in the background. Don't be stingy with paper or paint; paint ceaselessly, always choosing subjects from life. Don't put off until tomorrow a landscape that you can do today, for that landscape will never be the same again, it is ever-changing, as the angle of the sun, the weather and the seasons change.

"The ability to paint in watercolors," says Aldo Raimondi, "is a gift of Nature." Let me add: try to discover if you have this gift. If you do, don't waste time, get to work with humility and dedicate at least three hours a day to watercolor painting.

Aldo Raimondi: Seascape at Sibenik, *1980, 23⅝×31½ in. (60×80 cm), Private collection.*

A landscape viewed from above

Never be tempted to work from photographs. Leave this type of copying to illustrators who, for professional reasons or lack of time, are forced to give up drawing from life and must copy from photographs or other graphic works.

Many painters do use photographs. Some even project a photograph directly on to the canvas or paper and trace the image. But don't be seduced into this way of working. It is better to fail a thousand times before obtaining a satisfactory result than to obtain acceptable results quickly but without improvement.

Look closely at this watercolor of a hillside village, that I painted in early autumn, when the sun had dissipated the early morning mists. It is reproduced in the same size as the original. The landscape is painted from above (it is almost a bird's-eye view) and the colors create a damp and suffused atmosphere, typical of the autumn season.

I will describe how the picture was painted, starting at the top.

The greenish background behind the houses is a mixture of Emerald Green and Raw Sienna applied with very free, superimposed brush strokes.

The trees and bushes were painted with Emerald Green, Burnt Sienna, Ultramarine Blue, and a touch of Carmine.

I used the same color to paint the dark areas and, when the paint was dry, I superimposed hatching strokes.

To paint the roofs I used Burnt Sienna, with Raw Umber added in varying quantities for the lighter and darker areas. Bistre has been used for the walls of the houses, and for the darker areas I added Ultramarine Blue. The parts of the walls that are in the light have been painted in Burnt Sienna with a little heavily diluted Bistre. The foliage in the foreground is Emerald Green blended with Raw Sienna; for the shadows I added Ultramarine Blue.

For the ground I used a well-diluted wash of Burnt Sienna over the Bistre.

In this painting I have used a hatching technique to convey the shape of the foliage. For the misty areas I preferred to use a technique of superimposed stains. I used semi-rough paper stretched on a board. For a different effect you could use the same method of painting, but using a rough paper, and if you want to alter the mood of the painting try using pale yellow paper and paint the same landscape at a different time of day.

151

USEFUL INFORMATION

Using acrylics as watercolors

The use of acrylic paint has increased greatly in the last twenty years, creating a new way of painting that is now widely known and accepted. Acrylic paints are used by artists, designers, art teachers, illustrators, and students as well as by amateurs and beginners who are attracted by their ease of use. By adding the right medium and diluting the paint with a lot of water you can obtain very much the same effects as you get with watercolors.

To obtain with acrylics the opacity of watercolors you need to add a special diluting agent that doesn't reduce the brilliance of the colors. The more water you add, the more transparent the acrylics become. As acrylics are water repellent you can easily superimpose one layer over another without the colors blending.

To get a blotchy effect with one large drop of color you must work quickly; once the color is dry it is impossible to work with it again.

Do not work with acrylics at a temperature below 10°C (50°F) because the properties of the paint are altered at lower temperatures.

You should also be careful how you handle finished paintings at temperatures below 10°C (50°F), because cold causes the layer of acrylic to harden, making it fragile. Raising the temperature will bring the paint back to normal.

To obtain an effect like watercolors, mix a preparation of water and opaque medium in equal parts, 1 to 1, then dilute one part of paint with two parts of the preparation. If the paint is not sufficiently transparent, add more of the preparation.

When acrylics dry they form a waterproof and flexible film. Because of this flexibility the paint does not crack when the painting (on paper or canvas) is rolled up. The film doesn't discolor or harden with time and colors are less liable to fade when exposed to light. With acrylics you can use sable-hair or synthetic brushes, but since the colors dry quickly it is very important to keep your brushes moist and to rinse them thoroughly in water when you have finished work.

To delay the drying time of acrylic paints you can add an acrylic retarding agent which is mixed with the color in the ratio of 1 to 3.

Watercolor media

There are on the market a number of liquid solvents and varnishes which can be added to watercolor paint to obtain a great variety of effects.

Winsor and Newton, for instance, produce a range of such products to meet all the artist's needs. With the solvents one can alter both the consistency and characteristics of the paint. While one doesn't usually varnish a watercolor, special varnishes have been produced as a means of protecting watercolor paintings from atmospheric damage and scratching.

The most commonly used products are:

Artists' acrylic gel medium: a transparent paste of average consistency that increases transparency and brilliancy and gives the paint a textured quality. It dries quickly, leaving a water-resistant film. It is not generally diluted.

Artists' acrylic gloss medium: a milky white liquid that increases the gloss, fluidity, and transparency of the watercolors. It dries quickly, leaving a transparent film. Do not dilute with water.

Artists' acrylic matt medium: a transparent liquid that thins the paint without reducing the strength of the color, allowing very thin, even washes to be applied. It dries quickly, leaving an even film. Do not dilute with water.

Gum arabic: a pale, rubbery solution that increases lucidity and transparency. Dilute with water.

Gum water: a pale gummy solution that increases brilliancy and transparency with an increase in fluidity. Dilute with water.

Nacryl acrylic medium: a transparent paste that increases the transparency, brilliancy, and gloss. Paint mixed with this medium will not be water-soluble once it has dried. Quick-drying. Dilute with water.

Ox-gall liquid: a pale, odorless, colorless liquid that increases the paint's fluidity, moisture, and adhesion of the colors. Dilute with water.

Art masking fluid: useful for covering the areas that must be protected when the paint is applied over an extended area. It forms a waterproof film which can be removed with an eraser.

Preserving and storing

Watercolor paintings are very delicate, therefore certain steps should be taken to keep them in good condition.

Apply a normal drawing fixative to the finished painting. Don't expose it to direct sunlight, otherwise the colors will quickly fade. Keep the painting away from damp, which can cause mould and may alter the coloring.

When framing a watercolor under glass, wax a sheet of brown paper (you can use floor wax) the same size as the painting and apply this at the back of the painting in the frame. The brown paper will protect the painting from contact with a wall that may be damp.

If after a few years you notice that a dark film has formed over the painting, crumble a piece of bread over the entire sheet and rub lightly with the tips of the fingers until the bread is gray.

Never use an eraser — even the softest type will leave marks. Greasy stains can be removed with a wad of cotton wool soaked in benzine. Work very gently until the stains have disappeared.

If, on the other hand, a stain from another paint has ruined your watercolor you must take drastic action, using a hard eraser such as a typist's eraser.

Sharpen one end of the eraser with a knife and then rub over the stain very delicately, trying not to erase any other part of the painting.

Mix the color or colors you used to paint that area and retouch the part you have erased with a very finely pointed brush which you will use to dab the color gently on to the paper.

This operation takes time and patience, and you will need to work meticulously and without hurrying.

If you don't want to frame your paintings you can store them safely in folders. Use stiff cardboard or plastic folders and place sheets of tissue paper between each painting to protect your works.

Remember that the folders should always be stored flat.

One last piece of advice: your watercolors should always be signed, in pencil, in the bottom right-hand corner.

INDEX

Picture Credits

Gruppo Editoriale Fabbri archives: pages 10, 13, 14, 15, 24, 44,
46, 50, 51, 60, 62, 71, 73, 77, 85, 86, 105, 107, 108, 109, 111, 113,
137, 145
Maimeri: page 9 (fig. 4)
Winsor & Newton: pages 9 (figs. 5 & 6), 11, 12, 16, 17, 18, 19, 153
Aldo Raimondi: pages 101, 130, 149
Photographs not otherwise credited were provided by the author

159

Production Services by Studio Asterisco, Milan
Printed in Italy by Gruppo Editoriale Fabbri, S.p.A, Milan